THE SOM d DORSET JOINT RAILWAY

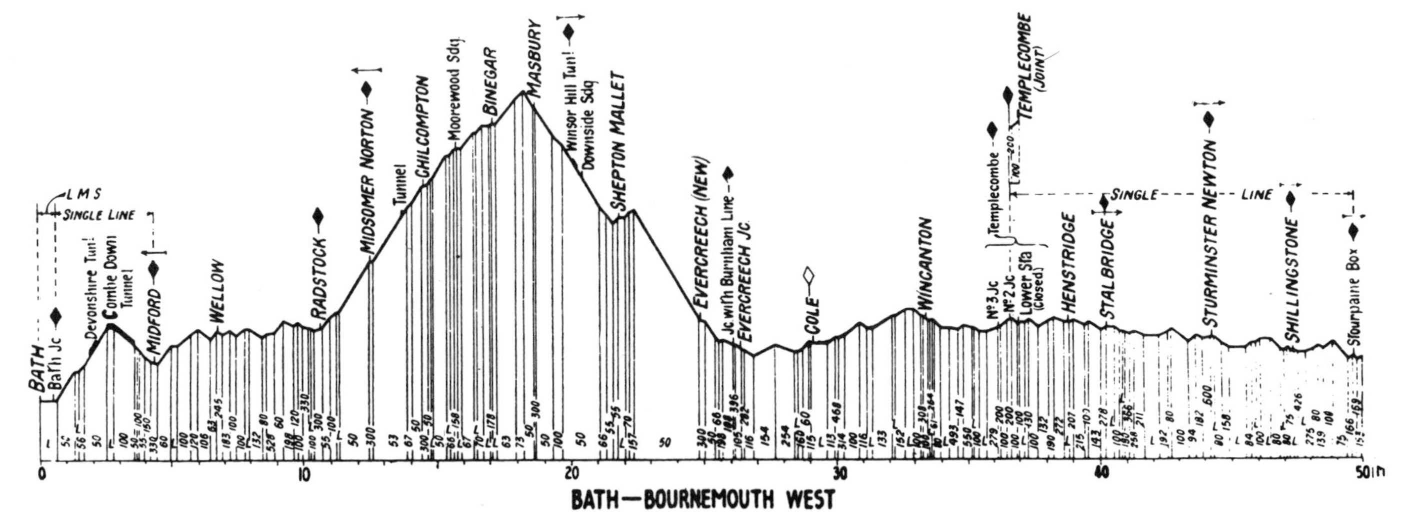

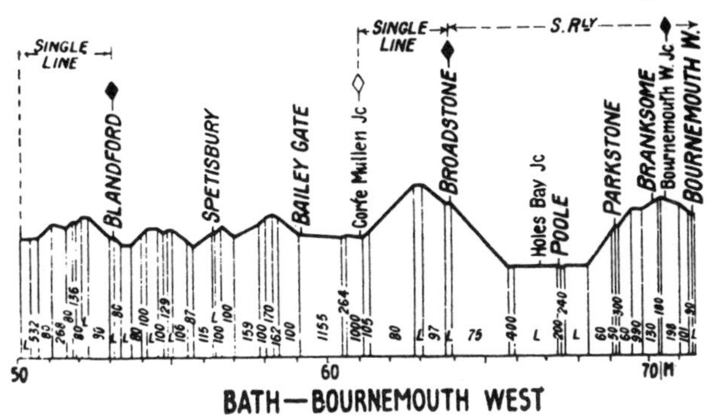

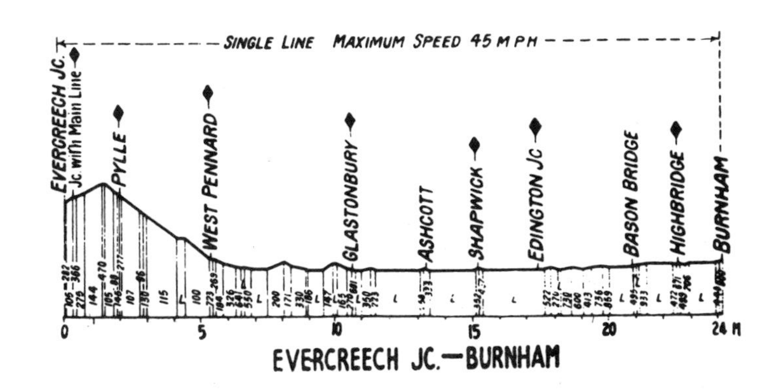

gradient profiles by permission of The Railway Magazine.

SUMMER EVENING ON THE SOMERSET AND DORSET – With the evening shadows lengthening, 9F No. 92245 draws near to Wellow with the 'Up Mail' on a glorious evening in early August.

2nd August, 1962.

The Somerset and Dorset in the 'Sixties

'DAVID and GOLIATH'. 2P 4-4-0 No. 40569 and 9F 2-10-0 No. 92006 coming up to Masbury Summit in majestic style with the up "Pines Express".

9th September, 1961

The Somerset and Dorset in the 'Sixties

PART 3
1960~1962

by
Ivo Peters B.E.M.

Oxford Publishing Co.

The Somerset & Dorset in the Sixties
Part 3 1960–1962 (ISBN 0 86093 160 9)

Reprinted 1984 and 1986.

Part 4 1963–1966 (ISBN 0 86093 161 7)

Reprinted 1986

This edition published 1990

A FOULIS-OPC Railway Book

British Library Cataloguing in Publication Data
Peters, Ivo
The Somerset and Dorset in the sixties.
1. South-West England. Railway services. British Rail. Somerset & Dorset Joint line. Steam locomotives, history
I. Title II. Somerset and Dorset in the Fifties. Vol. 3–4
625.26109423

ISBN 0-86093-490-X

Library of Congress catalog card number
90-81473

Published by:
Haynes Publishing Group
Sparkford, Near Yeovil, Somerset. BA22 7JJ

Haynes Publications Inc.
861 Lawrence Drive, Newbury Park, California 91320, USA.

Printed by: J.H. Haynes & Co. Ltd

Foreword

I am delighted to have the opportunity to introduce this combined edition of Ivo Peters' two books featuring *The Somerset & Dorset in the Sixties*. These two albums, together with the companion books featuring the S&D in the Fifties, form the finest pictorial record ever made of any of the former railway lines of Britain. There can be little doubt that the current interest in the S&D, as shown by so many enthusiasts is, in no small measure, a tribute to Ivo's 'camera-artistry', as so superbly portrayed in what has become acclaimed as the classic picture history of the line.

When OPC advised me of their proposal to produce this omnibus edition, I was asked if two colour photographs could be obtained to illustrate the dust jacket. Ivo, of course, never took a single still photograph of the S&D in colour, and so my thoughts turned immediately to his late friend, Norman Lockett. Over a period of many years, Norman frequently accompanied Ivo on lineside excursions, as is evident by Norman appearing in several of the photographs featured within the pages of this book.

I am most grateful to Norman Lockett's son, David, for agreeing so readily, to allow me to select two of his father's superb colour transparencies. From the extensive choice of material made available, I have selected a photograph taken at Masbury Summit; for this was Ivo's favourite S&D lineside location where, in accordance with his wishes, his ashes now rest at a spot where he had taken so many photographs. The second colour photograph features Midford; *my* favourite location, and one which Ivo readily admitted "ran Masbury Summit a close second!".

It was during the early days whilst preparing the first book featuring *The Somerset & Dorset in the Sixties*, that Ivo was suddenly taken very seriously ill. For some years previously, I had spent many hours observing, and therefore hoping to learn from his undoubted talent, as to how Ivo set about selecting photographs and putting together one of his albums. It was about this time when, one day, Ivo pronounced that he was 'nominating' me as his understudy; to be ready to complete the series of books, if necessary. As I have previously recounted elsewhere, that 'pronouncement' by Ivo met with my mixed reaction; on the one hand, surprised delight that amongst his many friends Ivo was prepared to entrust me with the completion of this important work, whilst, on the other hand, the uncertainty as to whether I could meet the challenge! Thankfully, I was not put to the test, for against medical prediction and due to his self-determination, Ivo was able to complete both of the "1960's" albums.

As always, Ivo went to immense trouble to ensure that his photographs were correctly trimmed and balanced. Then followed the preparation of the accompanying captions which, in addition to being fully informative and grammatically correct, had to be so phrased in order to be understood at the first time of reading. If not, they were rejected immediately, and rewritten. Finally, came the matter of page layouts; the all-important juxtaposition of pictures and text.

It was because Ivo expended so much time and effort to achieve only the best standard that he became so disappointed on those occasions when a publisher failed to match his original work. Such a case in point arose with the publication of one of the books which now features as part of this combined edition. For no apparent reason, the publisher enlarged several of Ivo's prints whilst maintaining the original overall plate size. As a result, the 'balance' of these pictures, so carefully planned by Ivo, was destroyed with, for example, a signal post 'decapitated', or a tree at the extreme edge of the print, which Ivo had deliberately included to 'take the eye around the picture', now omitted! In addition, the publisher made some minor, but totally unnecessary, changes to the original text. I hasten to clarify that the OPC imprint was, at that time, in other ownership, and that the present publisher – The Haynes Publishing Group – has very kindly agreed to correct the errors and amend the text so that all now appears exactly as submitted originally by Ivo.

Having regard to such previous disappointments, Ivo was somewhat apprehensive when, following acquisition of the OPC imprint, the Haynes Group informed him of their intention to reprint two of his earlier albums; *Somewhere Along the Line* (which Ivo considered to be his 'best' book), and *The Somerset & Dorset: An English Cross-Country Railway* (the first of Ivo's books dedicated exclusively to his favourite line). Ivo's concern, however, was to prove totally unfounded, and I well recall a visit to his home one afternoon, when he bid me to open a bedside drawer. Inside lay a copy of both reprints, but I didn't need to look at them – the smile on his face said it all. "They have made a marvellous job, Mike". This, from Ivo, was praise indeed for a publisher!

If this combined edition of his *Somerset & Dorset in the Sixties* is produced with the equal care, and to such effect, I know that Ivo would have been more than pleased with the result.

Mike Arlett
North Bradley, Wilts
1990

Ex-S.R. Pacific No. 34041 "Wilton" sweeps up the sharp rise to No. 2 Junction, Templecombe, with the 9.25 a.m. (SO) Bournemouth West to Manchester, London Road.

13th August, 1960.

ACKNOWLEDGEMENTS

Shortly after I began putting together "The Somerset and Dorset in the 'Sixties", I was taken seriously ill, and I am filled with gratitude towards my friends who came forward with offers to help in any way they could.

So many people offered their assistance, that it seems almost invidious to single out any by name. But I wish particularly to express my gratitude to Mike Arlett, who agreed to be my 'understudy', ready to complete the work if necessary, and who has spent many hours listening to my ideas and studying my choice of pictures and layouts. I have had unstinting help from Peter Smith and Peter Pike – both ex-S&D personnel – who have provided information and checked technical details, Derek Mercer and Peter Skelton have gone to great trouble to get the best possible prints from my negatives. As with all my books, Angela O'Shea has been of immense help with her constructive criticism of my choice of pictures, and the wording of the captions. And, once again, Peggy Leitch has kindly undertaken the tedious task of deciphering my illegible handwriting and typing my manuscript.

Finally, I express my most sincere thanks to my publisher, Oxford Publishing Co. for allowing me to do all my own picture arrangements and layouts. If some of the pictures contain too much 'countryside' for your liking, don't blame the publishers – The pictures have all been reproduced exactly as submitted by me.

The train times quoted throughout this book are from the Working Time Table. (SO) after a train time indicates that the train ran only on Saturdays during the summer service.

Ex-G.W.R. 0-6-0 pannier tank No. 3742 banking diligently at the rear, as the 11.00 a.m. down goods is swallowed up by Devonshire Tunnel.

26th June, 1962.

9F No. 92001 passing over Cole viaduct with the 'Up Mail' on a fine evening in early August.

7th August, 1962.

INTRODUCTION

As the 'sixties came in, the old order was changing fast for the Somerset and Dorset. The most apparent outward sign of this was in the motive power used over the line. Out were going the old, familiar types of locomotives which had served the S&D so well over so many years, and in were coming increasing numbers of B.R. standard classes, culminating in the dramatic arrival of the class 9F 2-10-0s.

By the late 'fifties the S&D, always an expensive railway to operate, was showing a very heavy deficit and it was obvious that drastic economies would have to be made wherever possible if the line was to survive. In 1959, spurred on by my love for the Somerset and Dorset and concern for its future, I plucked up courage and wrote to Mr. K. W. C. Grand, general manager of the Western Region, suggesting the use of 9Fs for working, single-headed, the heavy summer expresses which ran over the S&D. In my letter I outlined the considerable savings which could be made in manpower and operating costs if double-heading, then common practice between Bath and Evercreech Junction, could be largely eliminated.

The most I expected was a brief acknowledgement from a member of the general manager's staff. But to my great surprise, Mr. Grand replied personally to my letter, expressing interest in my suggestion and saying that he was putting the proposition to his motive power department.

Just what part, *if any*, my suggestion played in the S&D getting 9Fs, I know not. But I do like to think that perhaps my letter was the small spark that lit the '9Fs for the S&D' fuse!

So in 1960, following a successful test run by a 9F over the line in March, four of these immensely powerful 2-10-0s were allocated to Bath M.P.D. for working the heavy summer expresses over the Mendips, unassisted. Prior to the arrival of the 9Fs, the costly practice of double-heading between Bath and Evercreech Junction had been an indispensable requirement for any train of over eight coaches, unless hauled by an S&D 7F 2-8-0.

The 9Fs quickly showed they were capable of taking the heaviest trains over the Mendips unassisted. But to produce power of this calibre, called for a high rate of firing which had to be sustained over long periods; and this proved to be beyond the physical endurance of most firemen. So there were occasions when the maximum unassisted-load limit of 410 tons had to be relaxed slightly – and as a result, some summer Saturday expresses had to revert to being double-headed over the Mendips. Was consideration ever given, one wonders, to cutting out the assisting engines and instead, providing the 9Fs with two firemen between Bath and Evercreech Junction?

The bold move to use the 9Fs for express passenger work over the Somerset and Dorset was crowned with success. By the end of the 1960 Summer service, not only had they proved capable of hauling on their own – and with almost nonchalant ease – the heaviest trains over the line, but they had also established themselves as fast, free-running locomotives with remarkably good riding qualities. To this last aspect I can testify personally, for over the years I had the good fortune to be granted the privilege of an occasional footplate permit. I recall vividly my first footplate trip down to Bournemouth on a 9F. It was far superior to any other locomotive on which I had ridden. The smoothness with which the 2-10-0 rode through the succession of reverse curves between Midford and Radstock, astounded me – it was almost like being in a coach. And later on in the journey, when travelling towards Bailey Gate at an effortless 70 m.p.h., so quiet was the running of the 9F that the 'clickerty-click, clickerty-click' of the rail joints was all one heard!

With the ending of the 1960 Summer service the 9Fs were transferred away from the S&D, for unfortunately they had no steam-heating facilities and so could not be used on passenger trains during the winter months. But their absence was only temporary, for with the start of the 1961 Summer service, they were back again. For railway enthusiasts, however, the excitement of the 9Fs' return to the S&D was tinged with sadness when it became known that 1961 was to be the last year for the 2P 4-4-0s – a type which had served the Somerset and Dorset so faithfully for over 40 years.

But any feelings of sadness felt in 1961 were to be as nothing, compared with what was to come in 1962. It had already been learnt that, as in the two previous years, four 9Fs were to be transferred to Bath M.P.D. for the 1962 Summer service, when the shock news broke. After the conclusion of the 1962 Summer service, all through trains over the Somerset and Dorset were to end.

So unexpected and shattering was this abrupt announcement, that for many people, both professional railwaymen and railway enthusiasts alike, it took time for the full implications to be realised. No more "Pines Express", no more hectic summer Saturdays, and – fearful thought – probably soon, no more S&D. Tragically, this fear was to be proved correct. The Somerset and Dorset was closed in March 1966.

This book, which is the first of two volumes on the Somerset and Dorset in the 'sixties, covers the three years from the beginning of 1960 to the end of 1962.

Ivo Peters
1982

S&D 7F 2-8-0 No. 53808 standing in Evercreech Junction station yard, waiting to take over for the run up to Bath, an enthusiasts special which was traversing the Branch, hauled by an ex-G.W.R. 0-6-0.

This is the S&D 7F which is owned by the Somerset and Dorset Railway Trust and is in the process of being restored to running order at the Trust's headquarters at Washford on the West Somerset Railway.

30th September, 1962.

◁ The down "Pines Express" hauled by ex-L.M.S. 2P No. 40700 and ex-S.R. Pacific No. 34041 "Wilton" running through the Midford valley towards Wellow.

30th July, 1960.

1. In wintry conditions, S&D 7F No. 53802 drops down towards Midford with the 11.00 a.m. Bath to Evercreech Junction goods.
   This was the last picture I took of 53802 before she was withdrawn from service and sent to Works for scrapping on 4th March, 1960.
   16th January, 1960.

1960

THE 9Fs ARRIVE

The undoubted highlight of the year for the Somerset and Dorset was the test run over the line of a B.R. Standard class 9F 2-10-0. The trial was to assess whether these locomotives would be suitable for hauling, unassisted over the S&D. "The Pines Express" and the heavy holiday trains which ran between the Midlands and the North, and Bournemouth at week-ends during the summer service. The test run, carried out in appalling conditions on 29th March, was a complete success and as a result, Bath motive power depot was allocated four 9Fs for the duration of the summer service.

Although overshadowed by the 9Fs' arrival, another interesting locomotive 'event' was the allocation to Templecombe M.P.D. of a B.R. standard class 4 4-6-0, No. 75027. This was Templecombe's first Standard class 4 4-6-0, although Bath M.P.D. had had three of this type since 1956, and interest was aroused in December when one of these, No. 75072, arrived back from a general overhaul at Eastleigh Works, which included the fitting of a double blast-pipe and chimney. (Bath's other two class 4s were similarly modified in 1961).

On a sadder note, S&D 7F No. 53802 was withdrawn from service in March, and broken up. No. 53800 had met a similar fate in June 1959, so this now left nine S&D 7F 2-8-0s still in service.

The year ended on a dramatic note. During the month of November there had been day after day of incessant rain, and at the beginning of December, the area around Bath was subjected to the worst floods in living memory. The continuous, torrential rain caused a subsidence on the S&D just to the north of Midford Station, and the line had to be closed to all traffic from Sunday, 4th December until midday, Friday, 9th December. During this period, "The Pines Express" was diverted to run via Fordingbridge, Salisbury, Westbury, Bath Spa, Dr. Day's Junction, and then up to Yate, where it was able to join its normal route.

2. Mr. Harold Morris, the Bath shed master, standing beside No. 92204, the 9F which had been sent over from St. Philip's Marsh shed, Bristol, for the test run over the Somerset and Dorset.
   29th March, 1960.

3. Templecombe's new acquisition. B.R. standard class 4 4-6-0 No. 75027, setting off from Midford in charge of the 4.37 p.m. down local from Bath to Templecombe.

75027 differed from Bath's class 4s in being painted green, and she also had one of the smaller tenders. Happily 75027 has been preserved, and may be seen running, in immaculate condition, on the Bluebell Railway in Sussex.

19th April, 1960.

THE S&D's B.R. STANDARD CLASS 4 4-6-0s

4. Bath M.P.D. had been allocated three standard class 4 4-6-0s in 1956. One of these, No. 75072, is seen here standing in Bath, Green Park, station, waiting to leave with the 1.10 p.m. down local.

No. 75072 had only recently returned from a general overhaul at Eastleigh Works which included the fitting of a double blast-pipe and chimney.

31st December, 1960.

THE 9F TRIAL OVER THE S&D

On Tuesday, 29th March, 1960, a test run was made from Bath down to Bournemouth and back with a B.R. standard class 9F 2-10-0 to assess the suitability of these engines for hauling, unassisted, "The Pines Express" and the heavy trains which passed over the Somerset and Dorset line at weekends during the summer service.

The engine for the test run was No. 92204 from St. Philip's Marsh shed, Bristol. This was one of the last batch of 9Fs to be erected at Swindon and was built new with a double blast pipe and chimney. 92204 was less than one year old, having entered service in April 1959, and was in excellent mechanical condition.

The weather on the day of the test run was appalling, with high wind and driving rain, but the 9F, expertly handled by driver Bill Rawles and fireman Ron Bean, put up an outstanding performance, and as a result, four 9Fs were allocated to Bath M.P.D. for the duration of the 1960 summer service.

5. No. 92204 standing beside the coal stage on Bath shed. Southern Region locomotive inspector Jack Evans can be seen looking out from the 9F's cab. Locomotive inspectors from both the Western and Southern Regions travelled on the test train, taking it in turns to ride on the footplate.

29th March, 1960.

6. 92204 climbing vigorously up the 1 in 50 bank out of Bath towards Devonshire Tunnel with her test train of ten coaches and a van. Some idea of the appalling weather conditions can be appreciated from this picture!

29th March, 1960.

7.

(Left) On the down run a stop was made at Evercreech Junction for water. With the rain continuing to beat down pitiously, Ron Bean tops up the 9F's tender, whilst Bill Rawles checks round his engine that all is well.

29th March, 1960.

8.

(Below) Dropping down past Templecombe shed. The tablet had just been picked up at Templecombe No. 2 Junction Box, for the section to Stalbridge as the line was now single for the next 16 miles as far as Blandford Forum. – And still the rain poured down!

29th March, 1960.

9. The return run. 92204 stands in Evercreech Junction station taking water prior to the coming assault on the southern slopes of the Mendips. Conditions could hardly have been worse for the task that now lay ahead of them – the 8½-mile climb, much of it at 1 in 50, up to Masbury Summit, 811 feet above sea level.

29th March, 1960.

10. Cannards Grave Cutting. From Evercreech the line climbed steadily northwards at 1 in 50 for some three miles over the open hillside before reaching the start of the cutting up past Cannards Grave. A small lane bridged the line at the start of this cutting, and this was the spot I had chosen for my next picture.

Throughout the day the east wind had been increasing in intensity and had now reached near gale force as 92204 battled her way up the exposed face of the hillside. I heard her coming from far off, and although the train was still out of view behind a bluff in the hillside, great billows of white exhaust could now be seen sweeping rapidly westwards across the fields. Then just as 92204 appeared round the bend, she suddenly slipped furiously! But the quick reaction of driver Bill Rawles – an expert engineman – checked this immediately, and 92204, with sand on and now 'keeping her feet', came steadily up the 1 in 50 through the cutting, forging her way on towards Shepton Mallet.

29th March, 1960.

11. After taking picture 10, I drove rapidly up to Masbury, to see 92204 come thundering up through the rock cutting in tremendous style with her heavy train. Then, with a long imperious blast of triumph from her whistle, she was over the summit and starting on the fast 7½-mile descent of the northern slopes of the Mendips down to Radstock.
29th March, 1960.

12. Despite the appalling weather conditions, the test run had been a complete success. Back on Bath shed at the end of the day, driver Bill Rawles and fireman Ron Bean pose proudly for me in front of their engine.
29th March, 1960.

13.
92203 heading south from Midford with the 7.35 a.m. (SO) Nottingham to Bournemouth. This 9F has been preserved and may now be seen at Cranmore on the East Somerset Railway.
30th July, 1960.

THE SOMERSET AND DORSET'S 9Fs

The four 9Fs transferred to Bath motive power depot for the duration of the 1960 summer service were –

92203
92204
92205
92206

These engines, and all 9Fs allocated to the S&D in subsequent years, had double blast pipes and chimneys. If you saw a single-chimneyed 9F on the S&D, it had been 'borrowed'!

14. 92204, in charge of the 9.35 a.m. (SO) Sheffield to Bournemouth, running through the Midford valley near Lower Twinhoe.
30th July, 1960.

15. 92205 blasts her way up through Midsomer Norton in pouring rain with an excursion from Bristol to Bournemouth (9.36 a.m. off Bath). It was in conditions like this that S&D footplate crews came to appreciate to the full the sure-footedness of the 9Fs – so dramatically different from the S.R. Pacifics!
11th June, 1960.

Recently in the journal of a well-known railway society, an article on the 9Fs stated – "The 9Fs in particular are very prone to slipping . . .". With a 9F in the hands of an S&D driver, nothing could have been further from the truth.

16. 92206 heads the 9.55 a.m. (SO) Bournemouth to Leeds round the sharp curve leading away from Evercreech Junction North Box – and her footplate crew begin with confidence the 8½-mile climb up to Masbury Summit.
6th August, 1960.

17. The 10.30 a.m. (SO) Liverpool to Bournemouth, hauled by 2P No. 40569 and 9F No. 92206, coasting downhill towards Midford. In this instance, as in the picture below, the assisting engine is No. 40569, at that time "the flower of the flock" of Templecombe's 2Ps.

23rd July, 1960.

THE 9Fs WITH 2P ASSISTANCE

As explained in the introduction, the 9Fs could haul on their own the heaviest trains to run over the Somerset & Dorset. It was for the firemen's benefit that the 9Fs were provided with pilots when trains exceeded a certain weight.

18. 2P No. 40569 and 9F No. 92203 coming up to Masbury Summit with the 7.40 a.m. (SO) Bradford to Bournemouth.

18th June, 1960.

And on a Saturday morning in August – an amusing contrast at Masbury Summit.

19. "I wandered lonely as a cloud . . ." In response to an urgent call to Radstock for assistance, 'Jinty' No. 47275 gallops gaily over Masbury Summit as she hurries down to Evercreech Junction to assist an up express over the Mendips.

20th August, 1960.

20.
92204 demonstrates the outstanding ability of the 9Fs as with almost nonchalant ease – and starting to blow off – she threads the rock cutting leading up to the summit with the 8.16 a.m. (SO) Bournemouth to Liverpool.

20th August, 1960.

21. 73051 emerges from Combe Down Tunnel into Lyncombe Vale with the 9.45 a.m. (Sundays) from Bournemouth to Bristol.

3rd July, 1960.

IN 1960 THE S&D HAD A STUD OF 7 B.R. CLASS 5 4-6-0s –

73019	73050
73028	73051
73047	73052
73049	

For the duration of the summer service, these were augmented by No. 73087 on loan from Nine Elms Depot.

Every year, since 1956, Nine Elms had loaned the S&D two of their class 5s, Nos. 73087 and 73116 for the duration of the summer service. In 1960, 73087 had arrived at Bath as usual, but not 73116 which remained 'at home' at Nine Elms. However, during the year 73116 was seen occasionally on the S&D, for Bournemouth Central Depot was diagrammed to provide the power for certain trains up to Bath and back. 73116 was still fitted with a tablet catcher bracket from her 'S&D days', so if she happened to be on Bournemouth Central shed, and available, she would be used in preference for the Pacific normally rostered for the turn, and be sent over to Branksome shed to work the train.

22. (Below) 73028 – sadly in need of a good clean! – was one of the B.R. class 5s transferred to Bath M.P.D. in 1958 by the Western Region when they handed back to the London Midland Region, the S&D's last two remaining Stanier 'Black Fives'.
73028 is seen here running through the Midford valley with the down 'Pines' relief on a dull day in April.

16th April, 1960.

23. 73087, on loan to the S&D for the duration of the summer service, coasting down past the grounds of Midford Castle in charge of the 9.30 a.m. (Sundays) Bath to Bournemouth. The fireman can be seen inserting the tablet in the mechanical exchange apparatus, ready to be given up at Midford at the end of the 4-mile single-line section from Bath Junction.
3rd July, 1960.

24. 73050, assisted by 2P No. 40700, coming up to Masbury Summit with the up "Pines Express" on a pleasant Saturday morning in early July.
Happily 73050 has been preserved. Painstakingly restored, and kept in immaculate condition, she may now be seen running on the Nene Valley Railway, near Peterborough.
2nd July, 1960.

25.
No. 40700 climbing up through the deep cutting leading up to Chilcompton Tunnel with the 4.37 p.m. down local from Bath.
40700, erected at Crewe Works in 1932, was the last of the 138 L.M.S. – type 2P 4-4-0s to be built.
2nd July, 1960.

THE FAITHFUL 2P 4-4-0s

26. 2P 4-4-0 No. 40569 and 9F 2-10-0 No. 92203 emerge from Chilcompton Tunnel in charge of the 7.40 a.m. (SO) Bradford to Bournemouth. – A piece of rapid motoring resulted in a second shot of this train coming up to Masbury Summit. (Picture 18).
18th June, 1960.

27. No. 40634 and S.R. Pacific No. 34041 "Wilton" coasting into Bath with the up "Pines Express". Standing on the right by the water softening plant, is No. 40569.
No. 40634 had been built specially for the Somerset and Dorset at Derby Works in 1928, her S&D. J.R. number being 45. I remember seeing her when she was just a few months old. Painted in the beautiful S&D blue livery, with S.D.J.R. on her buffer beam and tender sides, she looked absolutely glorious.

4th June, 1960.

28. The up "Pines Express" passing Wellow on a lovely summer's day, hauled by 2P No. 40564 and rebuilt S.R. Pacific No. 34046 "Braunton".
In the background is the tower of St. Julian's church, Wellow, which dated from the 14th century.

18th June, 1960.

THE STALWART 4F 0-6-0s

In 1960 the S&D's stud of 4F 0-6-0s still included Nos. 44557 – 44561, built for the S&D. J.R. by Armstrong Whitworth & Co. in 1922, their original numbers being 57 to 61.

29. 4F No. 44557 – ex S&D. J.R. No. 57 – approaching Wellow with the 3.20 p.m. down local from Bath.

5th March, 1960.

30. Another of the ex-S&D engines, No. 44561, passing Charlton Marshall in charge of the 12.23 p.m. down stopping train from Templecombe to Bournemouth West.

3rd September, 1960.

31. S.R. Pacific No. 34040 "Crewkerne", assisted by 4F No. 44557, climbing towards Moorewood with the 10.30 a.m. (SO) Manchester to Bournemouth.

18th June, 1960.

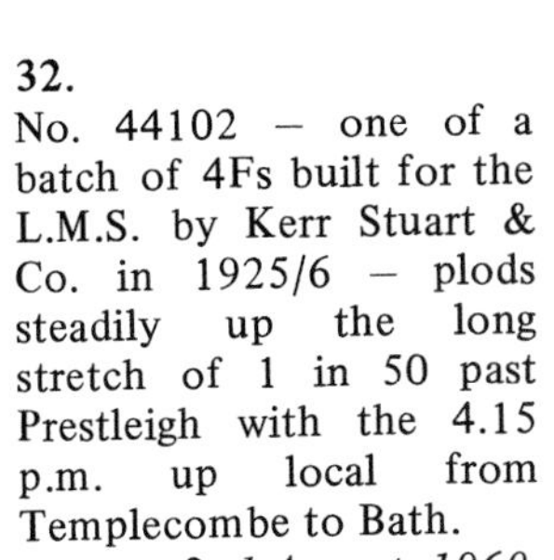

32.
No. 44102 – one of a batch of 4Fs built for the L.M.S. by Kerr Stuart & Co. in 1925/6 – plods steadily up the long stretch of 1 in 50 past Prestleigh with the 4.15 p.m. up local from Templecombe to Bath.

2nd August, 1960.

BOURNEMOUTH CENTRAL M.P.D. PACIFICS HELPING OUT ON SUMMER SATURDAYS

33. On a lovely summer's day in early August, rebuilt S.R. Pacific No. 34042 "Dorchester" climbs towards Binegar with the 8-coach down "Pines" relief. This was the maximum permissible load for a Bulleid light Pacific to take over the Mendips, unassisted.
2nd August, 1960.

34. The 6.57 a.m. (SO) ex Cleethorpes with eleven on and hauled by 2P No. 40634 and S.R. Pacific No. 34028 "Eddystone", comes plodding up through the deep cutting which led up to Chilcompton Tunnel.
2nd July, 1960.

35. Another of the rebuilt Pacifics, No. 34046 "Braunton" sweeps up to No. 2 Junction Templecombe in charge of the 10.35 a.m. (SO) Bournemouth to Manchester. With ten on, she would be having assistance from Evercreech Junction for the climb over the Mendips to Bath.

13th August, 1960.

36. Coming briskly up the long stretch of 1 in 53 towards Chilcompton Tunnel with the 10.38 a.m. (S0) Manchester to Bournemouth is S. R. Pacific No. 34041 *"Wilton"* – still in original condition – and B. R. class 4 4-6-0 No. 75027. Happily 75027 is still 'alive' and running, in immaculate condition, on the Bluebell Railway in Sussex.

9th July, 1960.

A SERVICE RESUSCITATED

After a lapse of many years, a through-working on summer Saturdays recommenced in 1960 between Exmouth and Cleethorpes, with a corresponding service from Cleethorpes down to Exmouth.

37. For the run up the Southern main line as far as Templecombe, the S.R. worked the train with one of their own engines which came off at Templecombe Upper to be replaced by an S&D engine. On this occasion, the Southern engine was U class 2-6-0 No. 31632 which is seen here at the old S&D No. 3 Junction, Templecombe, on her way to the S&D shed for turning and servicing.
No. 3 Junction used to have its own signal box, but in 1933 this was dispensed with, and the points and signals were then power-controlled from No. 2 Junction Box.
25th June, 1960.

38. S&D 7F 2-8-0 No. 53807, having taken over the train from the S.R. U class at Templecombe Upper, passes by the old S&D No. 3 Junction at the start of the run up to Bath.
25th June, 1960.

THE EXMOUTH–CLEETHORPES

As this train rarely loaded beyond ten bogies, the normal motive power rostered for this service over the S&D was a 7F 2-8-0, which dispensed with the necessity of providing a pilot engine for the climb over the Mendips.

39.
The 10.40 a.m. (SO) Exmouth to Cleethorpes comes round the tree-lined curves at Wyke Champflower, hauled by S&D 7F No. 53807.
9th July, 1960.

40. (Below) The 7.00 a.m. (SO) Cleethorpes to Exmouth running through the Midford valley on the last Saturday in July. As this was at the peak of the summer service, the train was loaded to twelve bogies and 7F No. 53801 had the assistance of 2P No. 40634 for the climb over the Mendips.
30th July, 1960.

41. 7F No. 53808 dropping down past the grounds of Midford Castle with the 8.20 a.m. (SO) Bristol to Bournemouth.
This is the S&D 7F now owned by the Somerset and Dorset Railway Trust, and is in the process of being restored to running order at the Trust's headquarters at Washford on the West Somerset Railway.
23rd July, 1960.

THE S&D 7F 2-8-0s ON PASSENGER WORK

As in previous years, traffic over the S&D line on Saturdays during the summer service was so heavy, that limited use had to be made of the S&D 7F 2-8-0s for hauling passenger trains.

42. As mentioned on the previous page, one working regularly rostered for a 7F was the Exmouth to Cleethorpes service. No. 53801 is seen here with this train passing Wellow Up Distant signal. The head-lamp over the engine's left hand buffer looks in a precarious condition – I wonder if it reached Bath safely?
Note the make-up of this train. The Exmouth to Cleethorpes service could be relied upon to produce an interesting variety in coaching stock.
23rd July, 1960.

53809 ON A *VERY* WET DAY!

This is the S&D 7F owned by Mr. Frank Beaumont, who bought her for preservation. She has been meticulously restored by a small, dedicated band of enthusiasts, and is now kept in quite superb condition at Butterley, near Derby, the headquarters of the Midland Railway Trust.

43. S&D 7F 2-8-0 No. 53809 climbing through Midsomer Norton in charge of the 5.40 a.m. (SO) relief from Derby to Bournemouth (9.25 a.m. off Bath). The weather conditions were terrible and no doubt 09's driver was pleased to have such a sure-footed locomotive in his charge. When handled by a competent engineman, slipping by an S&D 7F was almost unknown. *9th July, 1960.*

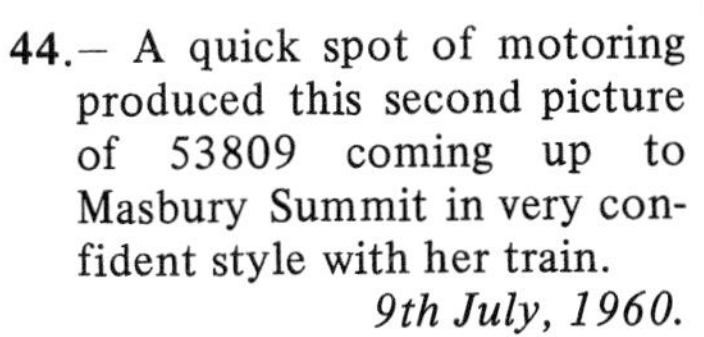
44.– A quick spot of motoring produced this second picture of 53809 coming up to Masbury Summit in very confident style with her train. *9th July, 1960.*

THE S&D 7F 2-8-0s ON PASSENGER TRAINS

45. No. 53806 dropping down the spur from Templecombe Upper and about to pass Templecombe No. 2 Junction with the 10.40 a.m. (SO) Exmouth to Cleethorpes. With eleven on, she would have had assistance from Evercreech Junction for the climb over the Mendips.

13th August, 1960.

46.
Another picture of the Exmouth to Cleethorpes, this time heading north past Wellow, and again hauled by 53806.

30th July, 1960.

47. No. 53807 swinging through the reverse curves towards Wellow with the 12.20 p.m. (SO) Bournemouth to Nottingham.

23rd July, 1960.

48. – Whilst shortly afterwards, at the same spot, 7F No. 53810, assisted by a 2P, appeared on the scene heading southwards with the 7.00 a.m. (SO) Cleethorpes to Exmouth.

23rd July, 1960.

– AND, MOST UNUSUALLY, A 7F IN TROUBLE!

On Saturday, 23rd July, S&D 7F No. 53806 was scheduled to work a relief from the North. On starting the climb out of Bath it immediately became apparent that all was not well with 53806 – she just would not steam – and she had ten on! After managing to struggle up the bank out of Bath, the driver stopped at Midford and urgent messages were sent forward to Radstock for a 'Jinty' to be ready, waiting to give assistance over the Mendips.

49. With regulator closed, 53806 drifts down towards Midford, where the driver was about to come to a stand beside the signal box to explain the situation, and ask for assistance from Radstock.

23rd July, 1960.

50. With 'Jinty' No. 47557 now attached as pilot, the pair come struggling up towards Midsomer Norton.

23rd July, 1960.

51.
The train approaching Chilcompton rock cutting. With both engines obviously being worked very hard, the 7F did appear to be starting to steam rather better.
23rd July, 1960.

52. At Evercreech Junction the 'Jinty' was able to come off. She is seen here 'having a good drink' after her exertions over the Mendips. The 'Jinty's' crew are driver Charlie Rawlings and fireman Dennis Love.
23rd July, 1960.

THE 7Fs ON THEIR NORMAL DUTIES

By the beginning of 1960, goods traffic over the S&D had already started to diminish as the Western Region's policy of diverting traffic away from the line whenever possible, began to 'bite'.
At the start of the year, no less than four of the 7Fs – Nos. 53801/5/7 and 10 – were temporarily 'in store' due to lack of work for them.

53. 7F No. 53806 running south from Wellow with the 11.00 a.m. down goods from Bath.
For over 80 years this train had been known as "The Burton" because ever since the late 1870s it had carried regularly much of the beer traffic from Burton-on-Trent to the southwest of England. But the Western Region, on gaining control of the Somerset and Dorset, had quickly brought this to an end, diverting the traffic to run via ex-Great Western lines.
19th November, 1960.

54.
On Saturday, 10th September, two ballast trains had been worked down the line to Binegar in preparation for reballasting work scheduled to be carried out in the area on Sunday. Both trains had been hauled by 7Fs – Nos. 53805 and 53801 – and before setting off, coupled together and with their brake vans, for the return run to Bath, the two crews had paused momentarily for me to take this picture of them.
10th September, 1960.

55. No. 53807, all 'spruced-up' for the occasion, comes up the bank out of Bath with the 11.00 a.m. down goods.
8th July, 1960.

AN S&D 7F ON A T.V. ASSIGNMENT!

On Friday, 8th July, BBC/TV came to the Somerset and Dorset to film one of the famous 7F 2-8-0s on a down goods for their programme, "Railway Roundabout".

56. – And, most unusually, the banker up to Combe Down Tunnel was also a class 7F (by special request!). However, the banker, No. 53801 – unlike 53807 – had not been specially cleaned, and was in normal rather grubby condition!
8th July, 1960.

57. B.R. class 4 2-6-0 No. 76015 and B.R. class 5 4-6-0 No. 73050 climbing up through Midsomer Norton with a Whit Sunday excursion from Bristol down to Bournemouth.

5th June, 1960.

EXCURSION TRAFFIC OVER THE S&D

In 1960 Bournemouth was as popular as ever with the public for a 'day-out', and considerable excursion traffic continued to pass over the S&D from the Midlands down to Bournemouth.

58.
These excursions were sometimes worked by Diesel Multiple Units. This one was forming the stock for an excursion from Cheltenham down to Bournemouth on a Sunday late in August, and is seen nearing Moorewood.

21st August, 1960.

No regular traffic over the S&D was ever diesel-powered. The Somerset and Dorset remained a 'steam' line to the end.

ENTHUSIASTS' SPECIALS

With the arrival of the 1960s popularity began to increase for running enthusiasts specials over the Somerset and Dorset. The organisers of these specials often made the request that, whenever practicable, the motive power should be an S&D 7F.

59. On Sunday, 11th September, the Stephenson Locomotive Society ran a special over the S&D from Bath down to Templecombe hauled by 7F No. 53804. On the down run, due to engineering work, the train had to run 'wrong-line' from Chilcompton to Binegar. In this picture, taken at Chilcompton, the special has just set back onto the up road. Walking back towards the train is the man in charge of clipping the points, whilst standing by the engine's front buffer beam, watching him, is the pilotman, waiting to climb on to the footplate as soon as all is in order.

11th September, 1960.

60.
In May, Ian Allan Ltd organised an enthusiasts special bearing the title "The Severn and Wessex Express". A part of the run was down the Somerset and Dorset and for this section the train was hauled by S&D 7F No. 53807, seen here standing in Evercreech Junction station taking water.

14th May, 1960.

BROADSTONE

61. After reaching the end of the climb up from Poole, 9F No. 92203 has just passed through Broadstone station with the 9.55 a.m. (SO) Bournemouth to Leeds, and is swinging left on to the S&D's own track which was single-line for the first three miles as far as Corfe Mullen.
In the immediate foreground is the line from Brockenhurst and Wimborne. The track passing straight through the station, ran to Hamworthy Junction.

16th July, 1960.

A RUN UP THE SOMERSET AND DORSET FROM BROADSTONE TO EVERCREECH JUNCTION

S&D trains setting off from Bournemouth for the run up to Bath, spent the first eight miles of their journey running over Southern track. It was not until they reached Broadstone, that the Somerset and Dorset's own line commenced.

BROADSTONE

62. On a fresh summer's morning in mid July, S.R. Pacific No. 34041 "Wilton", still in original condition, passes through the station with the 9.25 a.m. (SO) Bournemouth to Manchester.
16th July, 1960.

63. In sharp contrast to the picture above, the morning of Saturday, 3rd September, started off gloomy and overcast. (It was a job to get the needle off the bottom pin of the light meter!) Coming through the station is the 9.55 a.m. (SO) Bournemouth to Leeds hauled by 9F No. 92206. Note the mechanical catcher extended to pick up the token for the single-line section to Corfe Mullen.
3rd September, 1960.

64.
9F No. 92204, in charge of the 8.40 a.m. (SO) Bournemouth to Bradford, approaches Corfe Mullen at the end of the 3-mile single-line section from Broadstone.
The other track, which can just be seen behind the train, was the original Dorset Central line to Wimborne. When this was lifted in 1933, a short section was left in at the Corfe Mullen end to serve Carter's siding.
16th July, 1960.

CORFE MULLEN

65.
The 8.20 a.m. (SO) Bristol to Bournemouth, hauled by 4F 0-6-0 No. 44422, joins the single-line at Corfe Mullen. Ahead of them lay Corfe Mullen bank, 1¾ miles of 1 in 80 – and 44422 had 8 on! The fireman obviously had this well in mind and had been working hard, for the 4F was blowing off furiously as she swung her train on to the single line and started the attack on the bank.
Bath M.P.D. must have been in pretty dire straits for power if they had had to roster a 4F 0-6-0 for this turn. – Perhaps their usual expertise at 'borrowing' 'foreign' power had let them down this weekend!
Happily 44422 is still 'alive', having been preserved by the North Staffordshire Railway Society.
16th July, 1960.

BETWEEN CORFE MULLEN AND SPETISBURY

With no curves or gradients of any consequence, this was some of the easiest running on the whole of the S&D. The official speed limit was 70 m.p.h. – but if time was being made up, a rather liberal interpretation was sometimes put on this!

66. S.R. rebuilt Pacific No. 34042 "Dorchester", travelling close to the maximum permitted speed of 70 m.p.h., heads north from Bailey Gate with the 12.20 p.m. (SO) Bournemouth to Nottingham.

3rd September, 1960.

67. The 7.45 a.m. (SO) Birmingham to Bournemouth hurrying south from Spetisbury, hauled by B.R. class 5 No. 73087.

3rd September, 1960.

68. For the first few miles south from Blandford Forum the line undulated gently, short climbs being followed immediately by brief 'dips', some as steep as 1 in 100. In this picture, BR class 4 4-6-0 No. 75071, in charge of the 9.5 a.m. (SO) Bristol to Bournemouth, has just dropped down a brief stretch of 1 in 100 to pass beneath the small over-bridge just to the north of Charlton Marshall.
This gentle 'switchback' effect was hardly noticeable when riding in the train, but was much more apparent when viewed from the locomotive.

16th July, 1960.

CHARLTON MARSHALL

69.
9F No. 92205, hauling the 7.35 a.m. (SO) Nottingham to Bournemouth, starts to build up speed as she sweeps round a bend south of Charlton Marshall, near Spetisbury.

25th June, 1960.

70. Just south of Blandford Forum the S&D crossed over the river Stour. Passing over the lattice girder bridge on a bright July morning is 9F No. 92206 in charge of the 8.16 a.m. (SO) Bournemouth West to Liverpool, Lime Street.

16th July, 1960.

THE APPROACH TO BLANDFORD FORUM

71. 9F No. 92205, with Stanier 'Black Five' No. 44962 coupled ahead of her, draws near to Blandford Forum with a northbound relief to Halifax (8.00 a.m. off Bournemouth West). The 'Black Five', – a 21A Saltley engine – had been 'borrowed' by Bath M.P.D. to take a Friday night relief down to Bournemouth, and was working back up to Bath coupled ahead of 92205 to save having to find a separate light engine path for her.

16th July, 1960.

NORTH OF BLANDFORD FORUM

From Blandford Forum, for the next 16 miles up to Templecombe, the Somerset and Dorset was single track. Immediately on setting off north from the station, the line climbed at 1 in 80 for ¾ mile before levelling off in a lengthy cutting around Mill Down, and then starting to descend on a ruling gradient of 1 in 80.

All of a sudden the cutting would be left behind and the S&D was running through typical Dorset farming country with glorious views of the surrounding wooded hillsides.

72. Heading north with the 11.40 a.m. Bournemouth to Bristol, B.R. class 4 4-6-0 No. 75027, is just about to emerge from the lengthy cutting around Mill Down.
75027 has been preserved and is now running, in beautiful condition, on the Bluebell Railway in Sussex.
1st August, 1960.

73. The stretch of 1 in 80 up to Mill Down means little to 9F No. 92205 as, with her nine-coach August Bank Holiday excursion from Bristol to Bournemouth, she draws near to Blandford Forum.
1st August, 1960.

74. BR class 4 No. 75072, running on a slight embankment, rounds the long, gentle curve near Nutford Farm and starts to climb up towards Mill Down with the 9.55 a.m. from Bath down to Bournemouth.

1st August, 1960.

75. 1½ miles after her stop at Blandford Forum with the up "Pines Express", B.R. class 5 No. 73052 is getting back into her stride again as she heads north through the countryside near Nutford Farm.

1st August, 1960.

76. An August Bank Holiday excursion to Bournemouth, hauled by a B.R. class 5, running south through the lovely Dorset wooded countryside south of Durweston.
1st August, 1960.

AROUND STOURPAINE AND DURWESTON

77.
Ivatt 2-6-2T. No. 41296 with the 12.23 p.m. down stopping train from Templecombe to Bournemouth, running through a shallow cutting just south of Stourpaine.
1st August, 1960.

78. 9F No. 92205 heading south from Cliff Bridge with the 7.35 a.m. (SO) Nottingham to Bournemouth.
16th July, 1960.

APPROACHING SHILLINGSTONE

About one mile south of the village of Shillingstone the S&D passed through a deep, steep-sided sand cutting. At the southern end of this was a tall, attractive 3-arch bridge which carried a farm track over the line. This was numbered 184 in the S&D's bridge list and was known as Cliff Bridge.

An added attraction at this spot in summer time was the colonies of sand martins who made this sand cutting their home.

79. The 1.10 p.m. up stopping train from Bournemouth, hauled by an unidentified B.R. class 4 2-6-0, passes beneath the bridge.
1st August, 1960.

STURMINSTER NEWTON

This attractive market town, lying some eight miles to the north west of Blandford Forum, used to mark the approximate halfway point on the S&D's 16-mile length of single line connecting Blandford Forum with Templecombe. There was a crossing loop laid through the station and, as was usual S&D practice, the up road was given the straight run through.

80. 4F 0-6-0 No. 44422 sets off from Sturminster Newton with the 8-coach 2.45 p.m. (SO) Bournemouth to Bristol – a surprising assignment and a severe test for a 4F 0-6-0.
Poor 44422 was obviously having a very hard day! (See picture 65). One hopes for the fireman's sake, if not in the interests of time keeping, that something really powerful was waiting at Evercreech Junction to give assistance over the Mendips to Bath.

16th July, 1960.

81. The 9.35 a.m. (SO) Sheffield to Bournemouth hauled by 9F No. 92206, rumbles over the lattice-girder bridge which carried the S&D over the river Stour just to the north of Sturminster Newton.

16th July, 1960.

82. 9F No. 92204 is held in the down loop in Sturminster Newton station with the 7.47 a.m. (SO) Bradford to Bournemouth, waiting to cross the 3.40 p.m. up from Bournemouth to Bristol.
This crossing was scheduled for Shillingstone, but due to the late-running of the down train, control had altered it to take place at Sturminster Newton.

16th July, 1960.

83. B.R. class 4 No. 75073 with the 3.40 p.m. Bournemouth to Bristol, nears the end of the single line from Blandford Forum as she coasts up towards Templecombe No. 2 Junction Box. The 3.40 p.m. up was scheduled to call at Templecombe, so as soon as the rear coach had cleared the crossover by the box, the train came to a stand. The station pilot, 3F No. 43593, seen waiting on the left, then backed down on to the train and drew it backwards up the spur into Templecombe Upper station.

25th June, 1960.

TEMPLECOMBE

The 16-mile length of single line from Blandford Forum ended at Templecombe. The S&D was then double track for the next 32 miles as far north as Midford.

S&D trains calling at Templecombe used the outer face of the up platform of the Southern station. The S&D's own 'station', known as Templecombe Lower, consisted of a short platform on the up side situated just north of where the S&D passed beneath the S.R. main line. Templecombe Lower was virtually unused.

The procedure for S&D trains calling at the Southern station, known as Templecombe Upper, was most intriguing. Up trains, after leaving the single line section, came to a stand just beyond Templecombe No. 2 Junction Box. A pilot engine was then attached to the rear of the train and drew it backwards up the spur into Templecombe Upper station. When departure time came, the pilot engine, which had been un-coupled, was left behind in the platform, whilst the train engine – which had remained attached throughout these manoeuvres – set off with her train down the spur, past No. 2 Junction Box, and continued on her way northwards. Down trains calling at Templecombe Upper, ran up the spur and into the station. When the time came to leave, a pilot engine drew the train backwards down the spur to beyond No. 2 Junction Box. Then, as soon as the pilot had been uncoupled, the train engine – which, as with up trains, had remained coupled throughout – set off south with her train, picking up the tablet for the single line section as she passed No. 2 Junction Box.

84.

9F No. 92204, having arrived early with the 7.47 a.m. (SO) Bradford, Forster Square, to Bournemouth West, is held on the spur leading to Templecombe Upper station as the platform was still occupied by the 4.15 p.m. up stopping train to Bath.

25th June, 1960.

85. 9F No. 92204 was held only briefly on the spur before the platform became clear and she was able to take her train into Templecombe Upper for the scheduled call. Then, as seen here, the 9F and her train were drawn out backwards down the spur to No. 2 Junction from where they were able to recommence their journey down to Bournemouth.

25th June, 1960.

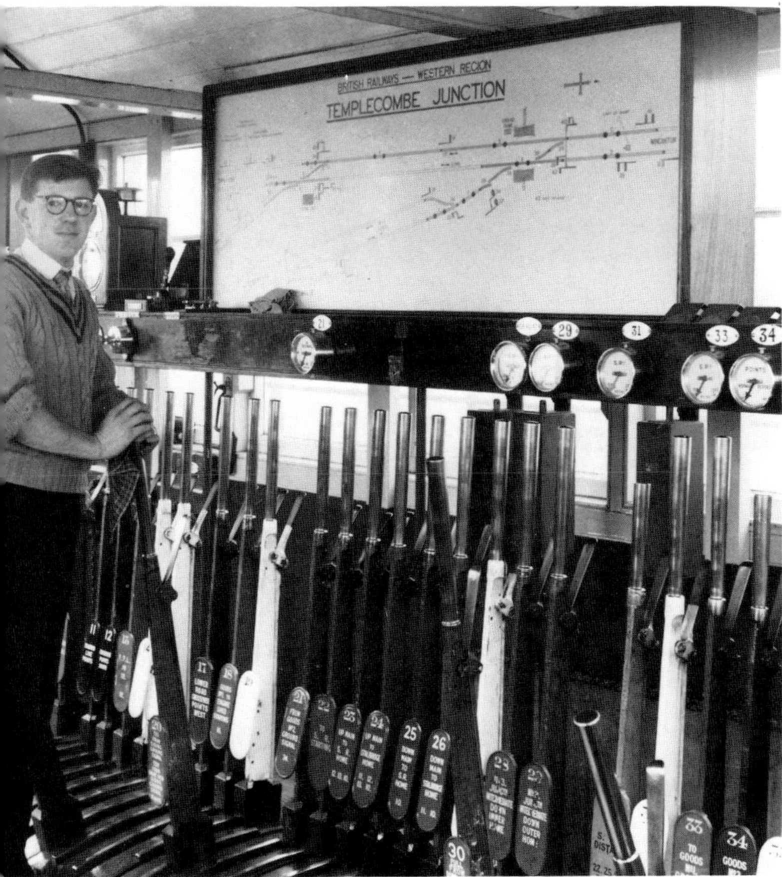

86. Signalman David Chapman on duty in Templecombe No. 2 Junction Box.

13th August, 1960.

87. Signalman Harry Bowles in Templecombe No. 2 Junction Box standing beside the Tyers No. 6 tablet instrument. The first section of the 16 miles of single line down to Blandford Forum was from Templecombe No. 2 Junction to Stalbridge.

13th August, 1960.

88. S&D 7F No. 53805, in charge of a relief from Bournemouth to Huddersfield (12 noon off Bournemouth West) sweeps up the sharp rise to No. 2 Junction where she will give up the single-line token from Stalbridge before proceeding on her way northwards.

13th August, 1960.

TEMPLECOMBE

89. 2P No. 40563 and rebuilt S.R. Pacific No. 34039 "Boscastle" with the down "Pines Express" – which was not scheduled to call at Templecombe – pass No. 2 Junction and join the single line which would now last for the next 16 miles as far south as Blandford Forum.
It was most unusual for the 'Pines' to be double-headed south of Evercreech Junction where the pilot engine normally came off after giving assistance over the Mendips. Presumably, on this occasion either the Pacific's driver decided he required assistance through to Bournemouth, or the 2P was needed at Bournemouth for an up working.

25th June, 1960.

90. The 7.35 a.m. (SO) Nottingham to Bournemouth was scheduled to call at Templecombe Upper. Hauled by 9F No. 92203, she is about to pass No. 2 Junction Box, and has the road to run up the spur into Templecombe Upper station.
25th June, 1960.

91. 'Jinty' No. 47542 and 3F 0-6-0 No. 43436 stand rather forlornly in the rain outside Templecombe shed on a very wet day in late March.
29th March, 1960.

92.
A line-up of Templecombe motive power standing alongside the shed. The presence of class 3MT Stanier 2-6-2 tank No. 40171 was interesting. Four of this class, Nos. 40098/126/161/171, were allocated to Templecombe in 1960, but their stay was very brief.
11th September, 1960.

93. Coming up the long straight from Lamyatt Crossing – just before the heavens opened! – 7F No. 53801 draws near to Evercreech Junction with the 10.40 a.m. (SO) Exmouth to Cleethorpes. Less than a minute after taking this picture, it was raining in torrents – and I was making a rapid dash for shelter!

27th August, 1960.

EVERCREECH JUNCTION

94. The crew of B.R. class 5 No. 73051, driver Donald Beale and fireman Peter Smith, in charge of the up "Pines Express", look out cheerfully as a 2P 4-4-0 couples on ahead of them to give assistance over the Mendips to Bath.

The 8½-mile climb up to Masbury Summit, on a ruling gradient of 1 in 50, started immediately from the platform end – a fact made very clear by the wagons seen on the left in the up yard which are standing on level track.

23rd July, 1960.

ENTHUSIASTS' SPECIAL

"The Severn and Wessex Express" organised by Ian Allan Ltd.

95. For the run over the Somerset and Dorset section of the tour, the special was hauled by one of the 1925 series S&D 7F 2-8-0s, No. 53807, seen here taking water at Evercreech Junction after the climb over the Mendips on the journey down from Bath.

14th May, 1960.

96. In bright sunshine, 7F No. 53807 sets off again with the special, past the tall water tower at the southern end of Evercreech Junction station, on the continuation of the run down to Templecombe.

14th May, 1960.

EVERCREECH DEPARTURES

97. 7F No. 53807 departs southwards from Evercreech Junction – but in *very* different weather conditions from those prevailing when picture 96 was taken! A cloud-burst was just ending as the 7F left for Bournemouth with the 9.08 a.m. (SO) from Birmingham. (See picture 93).

27th August, 1960.

98.

The Evercreech Junction station master, Mr. Stone, gives some last minute information to the driver of 7F No. 53808 just before he is about to depart with the 10.40 a.m. (SO) Exmouth to Cleethorpes. Standing in the middle road, waiting for the platform to become clear, is 3F 0-6-0 No. 43734 with the stock to form the 1.15 p.m. local over the branch to Highbridge.

2nd July, 1960.

99. Branch departure. 3F 0-6-0 No. 43216, in the charge of driver Charlie King and fireman Roger Parker sets off past the North Box with the 1.15 p.m. local from Evercreech Junction over to Highbridge. The train was being filmed for the BBC/TV 'Railway Roundabout' series, and I loved the 3F crew's sense of humour in having put up on their engine the B.R. express headlamp code!

8th July, 1960.

100. At Evercreech Junction there was a 56 foot turntable situated close to the North Box, in the 'V' between the main line and the branch. This was long enough to take an S&D 7F 2-8-0, but not a B.R. standard class 9F 2-10-0, which was one of the reasons why the 9Fs never worked any of the freight traffic between Bath and Evercreech Junction.
In this picture, S&D 7F No. 53807 is in the process of being turned. She had been filmed earlier in the morning for BBC/TV, when working the 11.00 a.m. Bath to Evercreech Junction goods – which accounts for her unusually immaculate condition!.

8th July, 1960.

101. On rare occasions, ex-L.N.E.R. engines visited Bath, working in from the north, but they had not run over the S&D since the end of World War Two. A B1, No. 61167, which had arrived earlier with a down express, is seen here setting off for the north, having taken over at Bath the 11.12 a.m. (SO) Bournemouth to Sheffield.

18th June, 1960.

INTERESTING VISITORS TO BATH, GREEN PARK

102. Since the Western Region gained control of the Somerset and Dorset in 1958, some ex-G.W.R. engines – in particular '2251' class 0-6-0s and various pannier tanks – had appeared on the S&D scene.

The ex-G.W.R. '43XX' class 2-6-0s were not permitted to run over the S&D but could work into Bath, Green Park, down the line from Mangotsfield. In this picture, No. 6384 is running in past Bath Junction with an enthusiasts' special – "The Severn and Wessex Express". (See also pictures 95 and 96).

14th May, 1960.

103. The re-routed up "Pines Express", hauled by rebuilt S.R. Pacific No. 34053 "Sir Keith Park", passing through Keynsham.
7th December, 1960.

DISASTER STRIKES THE SOMERSET AND DORSET "THE PINES EXPRESS" HAS TO BE DIVERTED

At the beginning of December, the area around Bath was subjected to the worst floods in living memory. The continuous torrential rain caused a subsidence on the S&D just to the north of Midford station and the line had to be closed to all traffic from Sunday, 4th December until midday, Friday, 9th December.
During this period the "Pines" ran via Fordingbridge, Salisbury, Westbury, Bath Spa and Dr. Day's Junction to Yate.

104.
S.R. Pacific No. 34105 "Swanage", still in original condition, standing in Bath Spa station with the up "Pines Express".
9th December, 1960.

105. After a busy summer Saturday, piloting expresses over the Mendips, three light-engines – ex-G.W. 0-6-0 No. 3210, in company with two ex-S&D engines, 7F 2-8-0 No. 53810 and 2P 4-4-0 No. 40634 – near Masbury Summit in the early evening on their way south to Templecombe.

12th August, 1961.

1961

THE SWAN-SONG OF THE 2Ps

For more than 40 years it had been almost an institution on the S&D that the pilot engine over the Mendips for "The Pines Express" and other heavy summer Saturday traffic, would be a 2P 4-4-0. But sadly 1961 was to be the last season when one would be able to enjoy this spectacle for as the year drew to a close, withdrawal began of the elderly, graceful 2Ps as additional B.R. standard class 4 4-6-0s were transferred to the S&D. A few 2Ps lingered on into 1962 on light duties and, rather surprisingly, the very last one to be withdrawn on the S&D, was an ex-Midland engine, No. 40537.

During 1961 the last four surviving 1914 series S&D 7F 2-8-0s were taken out of service after 47 years of hard work. There is little doubt that their enforced use on passenger trains – and the fast running which this entailed – on Summer Saturdays over the last 10 years, had shortened their life-expectancy.

With only the five 1925 series S&D 7Fs left, additional freight engines became a necessity. So in May a test run was made down to Evercreech Junction and back to Bath with an ex-L.M.S. Stanier 8F 2-8-0. This was a success, and as a result, engines of this class began to be transferred to the S&D as required.

Other locomotive news was the transfer to Bath M.P.D. in March of standard class 5 No. 73054 – recently repainted in lined-out green – in exchange for 73028 which returned to Bristol. And then came the expected 'high-light' – the allocation again to Bath M.P.D. for the duration of the summer service, of four of the highly competent 9F 2-10-0s.

One final 'happening' in 1961 was the change in the reporting number sequences used for trains on summer Saturdays. After years of the down "Pines" being '220', it now became '1095' – something frankly with which I found myself never able to come to terms.

106. No. 75073 pulls away from Midford with an up stopping train, past the site of the serious slip which closed the Somerset and Dorset for five days the previous December. (See pictures 103 and 104 on previous page).

15th April, 1961.

107. As in 1960, four 9Fs were transferred to the S&D for the summer service, and Bournemouth Central M.P.D. also helped out again with Pacifics on summer Saturdays. One of the 9Fs allocated to Bath M.P.D. for 1961, No.92001, stands ahead of rebuilt S.R. Pacific No. 34046 "Braunton". The 9F's driver is Oscar Pitt.

15th July, 1961.

108. B.R. class 5 No. 73087, assisted by 2P No. 40700 – the last 2P to be built (assembled at Crewe in 1932) – draws near to Binegar with the 9.55 a.m. down semi-fast from Bath to Bournemouth.

For the duration of the Summer Service, No. 73087 was transferred on loan from Nine Elms Depot to Bath MPD – as she had been every year since 1956.

9th September, 1961.

AN EX-L.M.S. STANIER 8F 2-8-0 IS TESTED OVER THE S&D

109.

The 8F trial took place on Wednesday, 3rd May. No. 48450 worked the 11.00 a.m. freight from Bath down to Evercreech Junction, returning to Bath with the 1.50 p.m. up freight off the Junction.

On the down run a stop was made at Shepton Mallet for the 8F to take water. Standing on the right are locomotive inspectors Lawrence Whitley (left) and Jack Hancock who were riding on the locomotive. With them (right) is Harold Morris, the Bath shedmaster. I was following the train by car, and much to my pleasure, Harold Morris had come with me as my companion on the trip. He was, of course, keen to see how the 8F 'shaped up' to the job compared with his S&D 7Fs. In the event, the 8F put up a first class performance.

3rd May, 1961.

110. (Below) On the return run, the 8F pauses at Midsomer Norton for a 'spot of shunting'. Watching from his box window is Joe Crouchen, the well-known and popular Midsomer Norton signalman.

111. The return run. The 8F climbing vigorously up the 1 in 50 towards Evercreech New.
3rd May, 1961.

THE ARRIVAL OF THE STANIER 8F 2-8-0s ON THE S&D

By 1961 the four surviving 1914-series S&D 7Fs were nearing the end of their working lives. So, following the successful test run over the S&D of a Stanier 8F 2-8-0, engines of this class began to be transferred to Bath M.P.D. as replacements for the ageing S&D 7Fs as they were withdrawn from service.

Sadly, none of the 1914-series S&D 7Fs survived in service to the end of the year. No. 53800 had already been withdrawn in 1959 and No. 53802 followed in 1960. The remaining four ended their days as follows –

Engine number	*Date taken out of service*	*Date to Works for scrapping*
53801	12th June 1961.	20th June 1961.
53803	10th November 1961.	1st February 1962.
53804	24th November 1961.	1st February 1962.
53805	14th February 1961.	3rd March 1961.

112.
S&D 7F No. 53808 prepares to come to a stand on arrival at Bath with an up freight from Evercreech Junction.
25th November, 1961.

Although the 1914 series of S&D 7Fs were now virtually worn out and beginning rapidly to fade from the scene, the five 1925 built 7Fs continued to perform well. In addition to their freight duties they continued – to many people's surprise – to be rostered for occasional passenger turns on Saturdays at the height of the summer service.

7Fs AND 8Fs ON GOODS TRAFFIC

113. As 8F No. 48450 comes across Midford viaduct with the 1.50 p.m. up freight from the Junction, the crew look out to see if the single-line token will be picked up cleanly.
3rd May, 1961.

After the satisfactory test run of 8F No. 48450, two members of the class, Nos. 48436 and 48471 were transferred to Bath M.P.D. It must be recorded however, that 8F-running over the S&D was nothing new – except perhaps to the Western Region who only gained control of the line in 1958. 8Fs worked over the S&D during World War Two, and in post-war years were used occasionally for the through-working of special freights. For example, I have a picture – taken in pouring rain on 22nd February 1956 – of a fertilizer special from Avonmouth to Blandford Forum, coming up through Lyncombe Vale, hauled by 8F No. 48332.

A CONTRAST IN S&D PASSENGER TRAINS

Two pictures, both taken from the same small bridge which carried a farm lane over the line just south of Wellow.

114. Ivatt 2-6-2T. No. 41243 passes by with the 6.05 p.m. down local from Bath to Binegar which ran every day of the week except Saturdays and Sundays, calling at all stations en route.
28th April, 1961.

115.

The heavy 12-coach 10.05 a.m. (SO) Bournemouth to Derby appears from round the bend, heading north, hauled by two B.R. standard 4-6-0s, class 4 No. 75027 and class 5 No. 73019.
9th September, 1961.

Happily, 75027 has been preserved. Beautifully maintained, she is now running on the Bluebell Railway in Sussex.

THE LITTLE TUNNEL JUST NORTH OF MIDFORD

Officially known as "The Long Arch bridge", it was in fact a short tunnel, 37 yards in length.

116. B. R. No. 73047 emerges with the 9.30 a.m. Whit Sunday excursion from Bath to Bournemouth and coasts down towards Midford Station.
21st May, 1961.

117.

The 10.05 a.m. (SO) Bournemouth to Derby approaching at speed hauled by two B.R. 4-6-0s, Nos. 75027 and 73054. With the climb at 1 in 100 up through the mile-long, unventilated, narrow bore of Combe Down Tunnel lying ahead of them, footplate crews never dawdled over this section!
12th August, 1961.

118. 4F No. 44560 leaves Midford viaduct with the 3.20 p.m. down local from Bath to Templecombe.
25th February, 1961.

THE S&D's 'ARMSTRONGS'

In 1961, all five of the 4F 0-6-0s built for the S&D. J. R. in 1922 by Armstrong Whitworth & Co. – hence their universal nick-name of 'Armstrongs' – were still in service.

119. S&D 4F No. 44558, driven by Dennis Latham, nears Midford with the 6.05 a.m. up goods from Templecombe.
15th April, 1961.

THE S&D's "BULLDOGS"

The long and distinguished service of these veteran 3F 0-6-0s draws to a close.

120. 3F 0-6-0 No. 43216 – old No. 72 built for the S&D. J.R. by Neilson Reid & Co. in 1902 – draws near to Horsington with the 2.20 p.m. Highbridge to Templecombe local.
22nd July, 1961.

121.
Old 3F No. 43216 again, this time in charge of the 4.00 p.m. local from Highbridge to Templecombe, heading south past Shepton Montague on a lovely afternoon in late summer.
2nd September, 1961.

THE EX-G.W.R. "2251" CLASS 0-6-0s

By 1961 growing numbers of these ex-G.W. Collett 0-6-0s were in general use over the S&D.

122. As they slow for the Midford stop, Clifford Smith, firing 3215 on the 4.15 p.m. up local from Templecombe, suddenly spots a friend and gives a hearty wave.

5th August, 1961.

123. On a bright evening in September, No. 3215, again in charge of the 4.15 p.m. up local from Templecombe, prepares to stop at Shepton Mallet.

9th September, 1961.

THE FOUR 9Fs ALLOCATED TO THE S&D FOR THE 1961 SUMMER SERVICE

92000
92001
92006
92212

The Western Region's choice of 9Fs for the S&D for 1961 was an interesting one. Three of the engines were from the very first batch of 9Fs to be built, and included 92000, the doyen of the class. They were erected at Crewe in 1953, but since their construction all three had been modified to have the double blast-pipe and chimney arrangement. In contrast, the fourth engine, 92212, came from the final batch of 9Fs to be built, which were erected at Swindon in 1959/60 and had double blast-pipes and chimneys from new.

124. "Are the points right?!" Although I knew perfectly well that it was impossible for the points to be changed to lead into the goods yard, once the road had been given to an up train, yet whenever I took pictures from this spot, I could never stop myself taking quick, furtive glances at the points to make sure they remained set for the main line!

9F No. 92000, in charge of the 9.55 a.m. (SO) Bournemouth to Leeds, has just emerged from the short tunnel just north of Midford station, and is passing the small hut, 'Midford A'. which housed the ground frame controlling the points which led into Midford goods yard.

By the way, disregard the reporting number 1084 carried by 92000. This referred to the 10.28 p.m. (Fridays) Manchester to Bournemouth which 92000 had taken down to Bournemouth in the early hours of the morning.

12th August, 1961.

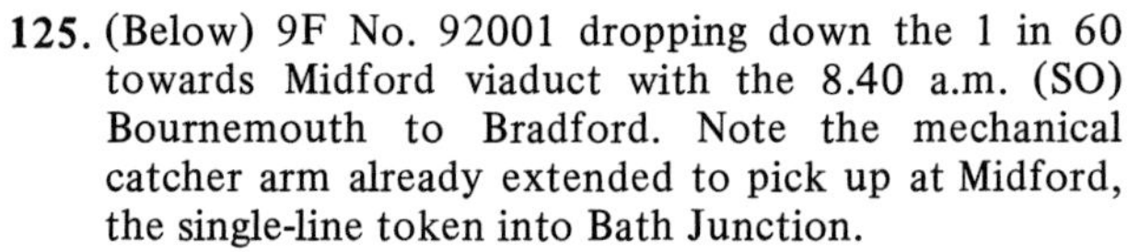

125. (Below) 9F No. 92001 dropping down the 1 in 60 towards Midford viaduct with the 8.40 a.m. (SO) Bournemouth to Bradford. Note the mechanical catcher arm already extended to pick up at Midford, the single-line token into Bath Junction.

8th July, 1961.

126. The 9.30 a.m. (Summer Sundays) Bristol to Bournemouth draws near to Binegar, hauled by 9F No. 92212.
18th June, 1961.

127. 9F No. 92006 with the 7.43 a.m. (SO) Bradford to Bournemouth, coasting into Shepton Mallet station where she was booked to stop for two minutes from 3.39 p.m. to 3.41 p.m.
5th August, 1961.

THE S&D's 9Fs

All 9Fs transferred to the S&D over the years were of the double-chimney type. – So if one saw a single-chimney 9F on the S&D, it was obviously 'borrowed'!

128. No. 92078 swings north at Broadstone on to the S&D's single line to Corfe Mullen.

22nd July, 1961.

'BORROWED' 9Fs

On no less than three successive Saturdays in July, Bath M.P.D. were successful in 'borrowing' a 9F for a run down to Bournemouth and back! All were of the single-chimney type and for the return runs back up to Bath, all were used on the same working – the 9.55 a.m. (SO) Bournemouth to Leeds.

129. No. 92152 emerges from the very restricted bore of Devonshire Tunnel, Bath. The clearance between the top of a 9F's chimney and the roof of the tunnel was less than one foot!

15th July, 1961.

130.
No. 92059 heading north from Wellow.

29th July, 1961.

INTERESTING VISITORS TO BATH, GREEN PARK, FROM THE NORTH

131. Rebuilt "Patriot" No. 45532 "Illustrious" arriving with an express from the North.

10th June, 1961.

132. The famous engine No. 46100 "Royal Scot", in the charge of driver John Stamp, leaving Bath with the up "Pines Express".

10th June, 1961.

133. As 2P No. 40569, piloting S.R. rebuilt Pacific No. 34045 "Ottery St. Mary", came into sight, drifting through the reverse curves near Lower Twinhoe with the 9.25 a.m. (SO) Bournemouth to Manchester, the train was obviously slowing down. Midford Up Distant had been 'on' and, with both engines blowing off and their regulators closed, the crews were expecting to be brought to a stand round the corner at Midford Up Outer Home signal.

12th August, 1961.

THE SWAN-SONG OF THE 2Ps

For over 40 years the 2P 4-4-0s had played a vital role in the working of passenger trains over the S&D main line. After the arrival in 1938 of the Stanier 'Black Fives', the 2Ps continued working the semi-fasts and local services, but perhaps one of their best known and traditional tasks was that of piloting heavy expresses over the Mendips.

Now, almost suddenly, we were seeing their last year in this role, for as the 1961 summer service drew to a close, so ended finally all 2P piloting. A few of the class lingered on briefly into 1962 on secondary duties, but all too soon, the last had gone – and the graceful 2P had vanished for ever from the S&D scene.

134.

2P No. 40700 and S.R. rebuilt-Pacific No. 34028 "Eddystone" appear from round the bend, with the 12.20 p.m. (SO) service from Bournemouth to Nottingham, and coast down the 1 in 60 towards Midford viaduct. No. 40700, erected at Crewe in 1932, was the last 2P to be built.

9th September, 1961.

135.

2P No. 40634 and 4F No. 44422 climb up towards Devonshire Tunnel, Bath, in charge of the 7.00 a.m. (SO) Cleethorpes to Exmouth. 40634 was one of three 2Ps built specially for the S&D at Derby in 1928. Her original S&D. J.R. number was 45 and when she emerged from the Works she must have looked magnificent for she had been finished in the very beautiful Somerset and Dorset blue livery.

9th September, 1961.

136. Shepton Mallet departure. 2P No. 40563 sets off with the 3.20 p.m. Bath to Templecombe local – a picture that shows well the simple and graceful design of the 2P 4-4-0s.

THE SWAN-SONG OF THE 2Ps

137. 2P 4-4-0 No. 40569 and 9F 2-10-0 No. 92000 at the head of the up "Pines Express" drift off the S&D single line at Bath Junction to join the Midland main line for the last half-mile into Bath, Green Park, station.

24th June, 1961.

138. 2P 4-4-0 No. 40564 and S&D 7F No. 53806 emerge from Devonshire Tunnel, coasting down the 1 in 50 bank into Bath with the 11.12 a.m. (SO) Bournemouth to Sheffield. Note the mechanical tablet exchange arm on the 7F, already extended ready to give up at Bath Junction, the single-line token which had been picked up on passing Midford.

9th September, 1961.

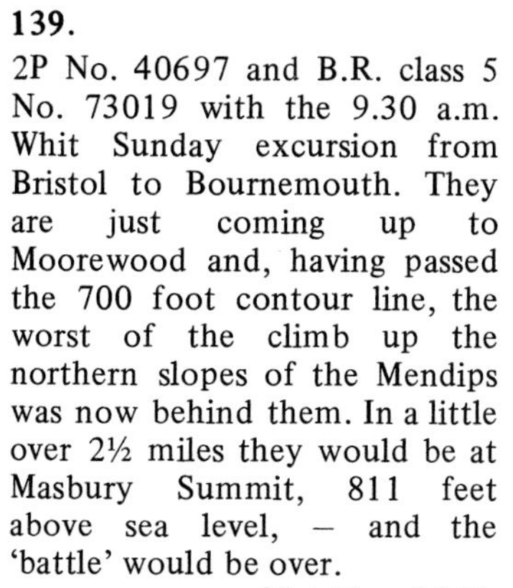

139.

2P No. 40697 and B.R. class 5 No. 73019 with the 9.30 a.m. Whit Sunday excursion from Bristol to Bournemouth. They are just coming up to Moorewood and, having passed the 700 foot contour line, the worst of the climb up the northern slopes of the Mendips was now behind them. In a little over 2½ miles they would be at Masbury Summit, 811 feet above sea level, – and the 'battle' would be over.

21st May, 1961.

140. On a fine afternoon in early August, 2P No. 40564 and S.R. Pacific No. 34043, "Combe Martin" – still in original condition – come up the final few yards to Masbury Summit with the down "Pines Express".

5th August, 1961.

BOURNEMOUTH M.P.D. PACIFICS WORKING OVER THE S&D ON SUMMER SATURDAYS

141. Rebuilt S.R. Pacific No. 34047 "Callington", assisted by B.R. class 4 4-6-0 No. 75027, climbing hard south of Binegar with the heavy, 12-coach, 10.55 a.m. (SO) Manchester to Bournemouth.
5th August, 1961.

142.
The down "Pines Express" again, this time hauled by 2P No. 40634 and rebuilt S.R. Pacific No. 34046 "Braunton", about to enter Chilcompton Tunnel.
8th July, 1961.

THE S&D 7F 2-8-0s ON PASSENGER TRAINS

Once again limited use had to be made of the S&D 7F 2-8-0s for working passenger trains on Saturdays during the summer service. But in 1961, only the five 1925-built engines appeared on these duties. Although two of the 1914 series – Nos. 53803 and 53804 – were still in service, they were in too run-down a condition to be used for this purpose.

143. S&D 7F No. 53810 leaves Devonshire Tunnel behind as she drops down the 1 in 50 bank into Bath with the 10.40 a.m. (SO) Exmouth to Cleethorpes.

9th September, 1961.

144. (Below) Ex-G.W. 0-6-0 No. 3210 and S&D 7F 2-8-0 No. 53806 – a rare locomotive combination – running north past Wellow with the 11-coach 10.40 a.m. (SO) Exmouth to Cleethorpes.

12th August, 1961.

145. – And another unusual combination. A 'borrowed' Stanier 'Black Five', No. 44771, and S&D 7F No. 53807, running down past the grounds of Midford Castle with the 9.03 a.m. semi-fast Bristol to Bournemouth. (9.55 a.m. off Bath). The 'Black Five' was not there to assist but was being worked down to Bournemouth to bring back a northbound relief in the afternoon.

29th July, 1961.

146.

S&D 7F No. 53808 running towards Wellow in charge of the 7.35 a.m. (SO) Nottingham to Bournemouth. The train was made up to ten bogies, which 53808 took over the Mendips unassisted – showing that there was still 'life in the old dog yet'!

29th July, 1961.

This is the 7F which is owned by the Somerset and Dorset Railway Trust and is being restored to running condition at the Trust's headquarters at Washford, on the West Somerset Railway.

A RUN SOUTH FROM SHEPTON MONTAGUE DOWN TO BROADSTONE

147. Ex-G.W. 0-6-0 No. 3215 passing by Shepton Montague on her way north towards Cole with the 4.15 p.m. up local from Templecombe to Bath.

2nd September, 1961.

148. The 7.43 a.m. (SO) Bradford to Bournemouth, hauled by 9F No. 92212, heading south from the tall overbridge at Shepton Montague.
This bridge, number 127 in the S&D Bridge List and known as Rock Cutting Bridge, carried a small lane linking the villages of Shepton and Stoney Stoke. It was unusual by S&D standards in the large clearance between rail level and the soffit of the arches which was 21 ft. 2 in. – vastly different from the very 'tight' clearances in all S&D tunnels and most of its bridges.

2nd September, 1961.

NORTH OF WINCANTON

149. The 7.00 a.m. (SO) Cleethorpes to Exmouth nearing Wincanton, hauled by 2P No. 40634 and 4F No. 44417. In 1960 this train, and the northbound Exmouth to Cleethorpes, was rostered for working by a 7F between Bath and Templecombe. Often loaded to only 10 bogies, this cut out the necessity of providing a pilot for the climb over the Mendips. But in 1961, with only five 7Fs left fit for use on passenger trains, the service was frequently rostered for a 2P and a 4F working 'in double harness'.

2nd September, 1961.

HORSINGTON

150.

One of Bath M.P.D.'s B.R. class 4 4-6-0s, No. 75072, passing Horsington with the 1.10 p.m. down local from Bath to Templecombe.
One could always tell a Bath B.R. class 4 from one of Templecombe's growing allocation because the Bath engines had double chimneys and the larger size tender. None of Templecombe's engines had either of these features.

19th August, 1961.

STURMINSTER NEWTON

– 8 miles south of Templecombe on the 16-mile single line run to Blandford Forum.

151. 9F No. 92000 standing in Sturminster Newton station with the 7.35 a.m. (SO) Nottingham to Bournemouth. The Working Time Table allowed for a stop here of six minutes – arr. 2.11 p.m., dep. 2.17 p.m. – for the purpose of crossing the 1.08 p.m. (SO) up from Bournemouth to Bristol. Looking out from the cab of 92000 is fireman Allen Northover.

2nd September, 1961.

152.
B.R. standard class 3 2-6-2T. No. 82001 arriving, light engine, from Templecombe.
22nd July, 1961.

153.
After calling at Sturminster Newton, B.R. standard class 4 2-6-0 No. 76062 emerges from the deep cutting just north of the station, as she resumes her journey with the 1.08 p.m. (SO) Bournemouth to Bristol.
22nd July, 1961.

154. (Below) B.R. class 5 No. 73087, in charge of the 9.45 a.m. (summer Sundays) up from Bournemouth, crosses over the river Stour north of Sturminster Newton.
27th August, 1961.

155.

B.R. class 5 No. 73050, hauling the 7.43 a.m. (SO) Birmingham to Bournemouth, passes under Cliff Bridge, situated at the southern end of the sand cutting about a mile south of Shillingstone. (See picture 79). Happily 73050 has been preserved. Excellently maintained, she is now running on the Nene Valley Railway near Peterborough.

22nd July, 1961.

SOUTH OF SHILLINGSTONE

156. S&D 7F 2-8-0 No. 53810 heading north up the long straight from Stourpaine towards Shillingstone with the 11.12 a.m. (SO) Bournemouth to Sheffield.

22nd July, 1961.

NORTH OF BLANDFORD FORUM

157. B.R. class 5 No. 73047 travelling at speed south of Stourpaine with the 9.30 a.m. (Summer Sundays) Bath to Bournemouth.

27th August, 1961.

158. B.R. standard class 4 2-6-0 No. 76009 rounds the long bend away from Mill Down as she heads north from Blandford Forum with the 1.08 p.m. (SO) Bournemouth to Bristol.

19th August, 1961.

CHARLTON MARSHALL

159. S&D 4F 0-6-0 No. 44558 passes the disused halt at Charlton Marshall with the 12.23 p.m. down local from Templecombe to Bournemouth.

19th August, 1961.

NEARING BAILEY GATE

160. The 9.03 a.m. Bristol to Bournemouth (9.55 a.m. off Bath) hauled by B.R. class 5 No. 73054, running south from Spetisbury towards Bailey Gate.

19th August, 1961.

BROADSTONE

161.
9F No. 92000, in charge of the up "Pines Express", swings north on to the S&D and the 3-mile single-line section to Corfe Mullen.
22nd July, 1961.

162. The 10.35 a.m. (SO) Bournemouth to Manchester, passing through the station hauled by S.R. rebuilt Pacific No. 34042 "Dorchester".
22nd July, 1961.

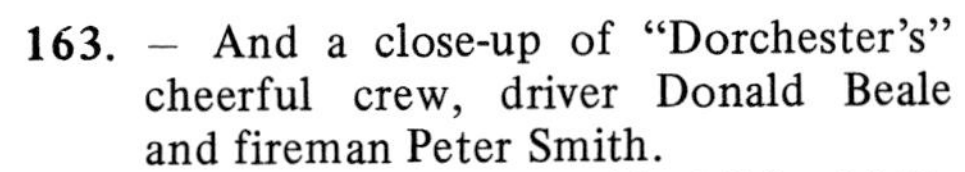

163. – And a close-up of "Dorchester's" cheerful crew, driver Donald Beale and fireman Peter Smith.
22nd July, 1961.

164. "Evening Star" standing on Bath shed on Friday evening, 7th September, specially cleaned up for hauling the last "Pines Express" to run over the Somerset and Dorset on the following day.

7th September, 1962.

1962

FAREWELL TO THE "PINES"

1962 saw the withdrawal of the last surviving 3F 'Bulldog', No. 43216, and also two of the 'Armstrong' 4Fs, Nos. 44557 and 44561 – the first engines of this class to go. As in the last two years, four 9Fs were again to be transferred to Bath M.P.D., for the summer service.

But these locomotive details paled into insignificance when the shock announcement was suddenly made that as from the end of the summer service, "The Pines Express" and all other through trains over the line were to be diverted away from the S&D. This news was absolutely catastrophic for the Somerset and Dorset. Almost overnight it was to be transformed from an important, cross-country railway linking the Midlands and the North with the South coast, into a line of little significance, running a purely local service. In the autumn of 1962 the Western Region had succeeded in reducing the Somerset and Dorset to a state of near impotence from which it would never recover.

165. The last two 1914-series S&D 7Fs heading slowly north from Bitton on their last journey. Both had been withdrawn from service in 1961. Now, on 1st February, No. 53803 was put in steam again and, pulling her 'dead' sister, No. 53804, made the melancholy journey to Crewe where both were broken up.

1st February, 1962.

166.
The sole surviving 3F 0-6-0 'Bulldog', No. 43216 – old No. 72 built for the S&D. J.R. in 1902 by Neilson, Reid & Co. – sets off from Cole with the 4.00 p.m. down local from Highbridge to Templecombe. Less than two months later, she was withdrawn from service.

30th June, 1962.

167.
On a fine Thursday evening in early August, B.R. 2-6-2T. No. 82004 makes her way leisurely southwards from Wellow with the 6.05 p.m. (SX) Bath to Binegar local.
2nd August, 1962.

THE B.R. STANDARD CLASS 3MT 2-6-2 TANKS

The Western Region introduced these engines to the line for working local services when they gained control of the S&D in 1958. Engines of this type were shedded at both Bath and Templecombe. In addition to working S&D trains, Bath often used theirs for locals over the Midland line to Bristol, Temple Meads.

168. With the 4.05 p.m Templecombe – Evercreech Junction – Highbridge local, No. 82001 comes up through the trees at Wyke Champflower.
14th April, 1962.

169. 9F No. 92233 setting off from the north platform of Bath, Green Park, station with the 7.35 a.m. (SO) Nottingham to Bournemouth. The start was fairly gentle because the train was about to take the crossover on to the down line.

8th September, 1962.

THE FOUR 9Fs ALLOCATED TO THE S&D FOR THE 1962 SUMMER SERVICE

92001
92210
92233
92245

As in the previous two years, all four were of the double-chimney type. In August 92210 was replaced by 92220 "Evening Star".

170. 9F No. 92210 emerging from Devonshire Tunnel with the 9.03 a.m. down semi-fast from Bristol to Bournemouth. (9.55 a.m. off Bath). Note that the Bath shed plate (82F) had already been removed in preparation for the engine's departure from the S&D, having been replaced by No. 92220 "Evening Star".

11th August, 1962.

171. 9F No. 92245 coming up to Masbury Summit with the 9.25 a.m. (SO) Bournemouth to Manchester and Liverpool.

4th August, 1962.

172. 9F No. 92001, in charge of the 7.43 a.m. (SO) Bradford to Bournemouth, coming vigorously up the bank towards Devonshire Tunnel, in the 1 in 50 climb out of Bath.

14th July, 1962.

"EVENING STAR" ON THE SOMERSET AND DORSET

On 8th August, 9F No. 92220 "Evening Star" had been specially transferred to Bath M.P.D. so as to be available for working on 8th September, the last "Pines Express" to run over the S&D. (See pictures 243–249).

173. The morning after – 9F No. 92220 "Evening Star" resting on Bath shed on the Sunday morning, 9th September. The day before, Saturday, 8th September, she had hauled, unassisted, the last "Pines Express" to run over the S&D.

9th September, 1962

174. After her arrival on the S&D, the first "Pines" to be hauled by "Evening Star" was the up train on Saturday, 11th August. This exceeded the load limit of 410 tons fixed for a 9F to take over the Mendips unassisted; so she had a pilot from Evercreech Junction, BR standard class 4 4-6-0 No. 75009, and the pair are seen here, climbing northwards from Winsor Hill.

11th August, 1962.

"EVENING STAR" ON THE SOMERSET AND DORSET

175. The last train hauled over the S&D in 1962 by "Evening Star" was the 3.40 p.m. from Bournemouth – the up 'Mail' – seen here approaching Midford in the early evening of Wednesday, 12th. September.
The following day, "Evening Star" was transferred away from Bath M.P.D.
12th September, 1962.

176. After calling at Templecombe Upper, and having been drawn out backwards from the station and down the spur, No. 92220 "Evening Star" sets off past No. 2 Junction Box on the resumption of her journey down to Bournemouth with the 9.55 a.m. semi-fast from Bath.
For the next 16 miles, as far as Blandford Forum, the S&D was single-line, and the engine has just picked up the token for the first 4-mile section to Stalbridge.
1st September, 1962.

177. Rebuilt S.R. Pacific No. 34042 "Dorchester" crossing over Midford viaduct with a relief to the down "Pines Express".

2nd June, 1962.

S.R. PACIFICS WORKING OVER THE S&D

In 1962, as usual, Bournemouth M.P.D. was most co-operative in helping out with motive power for hauling the many extra trains which ran over the S&D on summer Saturdays. But there was to be a sad feature about this year's operations, for it was destined to be the last year that there would be any necessity to seek help from the Southern Region. When the summer of 1963 arrived there would no longer be any extra trains on the S&D to be hauled.

178.

In damp and difficult conditions on a gloomy Saturday in May, driver Bert Brewer made an excellent climb of the Mendips with unmodified S.R. Pacific No. 34043 "Combe Martin" hauling an 8-coach relief to the down "Pines Express". In this picture, Bert Brewer and his fireman Peter Smith lean from the Pacific's cab as they come thundering up the 1 in 50 towards Midsomer Norton.

I must admit that, with the damp rail and the engine being worked very hard, I was expecting a violent slip from the Pacific at any moment! – But, as Peter told me later, she kept her feet and behaved impeccably throughout the 7½-mile climb.

26th May, 1962.

179. Rebuilt S.R. Pacific No. 34029 "Lundy" heading north towards Cole with the 12.20 p.m. (SO) Bournemouth to Nottingham.
4th August, 1962.

180. On this occasion the 12.20 p.m. (SO) Bournemouth to Nottingham is hauled by S.R. Pacific No. 34103 "Calstock", still in original condition. It is passing through the rock cutting at Shepton Montague.
1st September, 1962.

THE LAST YEAR OF "THE PINES EXPRESS" AND ALL OTHER THROUGH TRAINS OVER THE SOMERSET AND DORSET

181. The 9.45 a.m. Bournemouth to Manchester – "The Pines Express" – coming up to Masbury Summit hauled by B.R. class 4 4-6-0 No. 75009 and 9F 2-10-0 No. 92001.

4th August, 1962.

A selection of views of "The Pines Express" and some of the other through trains during their last weeks of running over the S&D.

182.

The 7.00 a.m. (SO) Cleethorpes to Exmouth passing Cole, behind B.R. class 4 4-6-0 No. 75009 and 4F 0-6-0 No. 44417.

28th July, 1962.

183. The 9.55 a.m. (SO) Bournemouth to Leeds climbing up towards Winsor Hill Tunnel. With 8 on, the maximum load for an S.R. Pacific to take over the Mendips, unassisted, No. 34043 "Combe Martin" – and her fireman! – were having to work hard.

11th August, 1962.

184.

Passing over Prestleigh viaduct, the 12.20 p.m. (SO) service from Bournemouth to Nottingham, is drawn by B.R. class 5 No. 73049 and S.R. Pacific No. 34043 "Combe Martin".

7th July, 1962.

185. The 9.25 a.m. (SO) from Bournemouth, nearing the end of a 3-mile stretch of 1 in 50, draws near to Shepton Mallet, hauled by 9F 2-10-0 No. 92245. For many years the 9.25 a.m. (SO) ex-Bournemouth West had run to Manchester, London Road, and Liverpool, Lime Street, and in 1962 the Southern Region Working Time Table *and* the Public Time Table, still gave the destination of this train as Manchester and Liverpool. But, for some reason which I could never fathom, the Western Region Working Time Table gave the destination of this train as Crewe!

30th June, 1962.

186. The 9.08 a.m. (SO) Birmingham to Bournemouth coasting downhill towards Evercreech Junction behind two B.R. class 5 4-6-0s Nos. 73024 and 73051. Heading north is B.R. class 4 No. 75009 which was piloting another class 4 with the 11.12 a.m. (SO) Bournemouth to Sheffield.

30th June, 1962.

187. The 10.40 a.m. (SO) Exmouth to Cleethorpes coming steadily up the 1 in 50 towards Winsor Hill Tunnel hauled by 7F 2-8-0 No. 53808. The S&D 7F's ability to take 10 coaches over the Mendips on their own (two more than the maximum unassisted load for either a class 5 or an S.R. Pacific) proved of great benefit on busy summer Saturdays when pilot engines between Evercreech Junction and Bath were in great demand.

11th August, 1962.

188. (Below) The 10.55 a.m. (SO) Manchester to Bournemouth, in the charge of B.R. class 4 No. 75027 and S.R. Pacific No. 34043 "Combe Martin", drawing near to Moorewood in the 7½-mile climb up the northern slopes of the Mendips.

14th July, 1962.

189. The 7.43 a.m. (SO) Bradford to Bournemouth heading south from No. 2 Junction, Templecombe. This train should have been in the sole charge of 9F No. 92245. For an amusing account of just how the Bulleid Pacific No. 34043 "Combe Martin", managed to get herself coupled ahead of the 9F, see Peter Smith's delightful book, "Mendips Engineman", page 65.

11th August, 1962.

190. The 11.12 a.m. (SO) Bournemouth to Sheffield making a rapid climb up towards Winsor Hill Tunnel hauled by a pair of B.R. class 4 4-6-0s, Nos. 75023 and 75009. Driver Donald Beale was in charge of 75009, which probably had something to do with the dramatic ascent being made of the southern slopes of the Mendips!

28th July, 1962.

191. "Royal Scot" class 7P No. 46157 "Royal Artilleryman", setting off in very determined style, for the run north with the relief to the up "Pines Express".
2nd June, 1962.

INTERESTING VARIETY IN MOTIVE POWER FOR TRAINS NORTHBOUND FROM BATH, GREEN PARK

Since the end of World War Two, there had been little variety in the motive power used by the London Midland Region for working expresses to and from Bath, Green Park. In the main, three classes appeared on these duties – the Stanier 'Black Five' and class '5XP' 4-6-0s and the Horwich "Crab" 2-6-0s.
Now, however, the L.M. Region's growing fleet of diesels was making surplus the more powerful types of steam locomotives previously used on the West Coast Main line.
One result – and a most welcome one for local steam enthusiasts – was the arrival in Bath on an increasing number of occasions of the "Royal Scot" class 4-6-0s. – But, to balance this, the "Peak" class diesels also began to appear on the scene!

192. A 9F 2-10-0 had hauled the 9.25 a.m. (SO) train from Bournemouth to Manchester and Liverpool over the S&D up to Bath. Now a type 4 "Peak" class diesel has taken over the train and is seen here setting off on the continuation of the run north.
14th July, 1962.

THE 2Ps HAVING FINALLY FADED FROM THE S&D SCENE, ALL PILOTING OVER THE MENDIPS WAS NOW DONE BY SIX-COUPLED LOCOMOTIVES

193. The down "Pines Express" passing Chilcompton, hauled by B.R. class 5 No. 73051 and S.R. rebuilt Pacific No. 34046 "Braunton".

23rd April, 1962.

194.
Stanier 'Black Five' No. 44841 ('Borrowed' from 21A, Saltley shed) and 9F No. 92233 climbing towards Midsomer Norton with the down "Pines Express". Travelling on the footplate of 92233 was the publisher, Mr. Ronald Nelson. The crew of the 9F, driver Donald Beale and fireman Peter Smith – keen to show off the prowess of their engine – were disappointed at having a pilot which they considered quite unnecessary, and before leaving Bath, asked for its removal. But unfortunately, Mr. Harold Morris, the Bath shed master – who would undoubtedly have agreed to this – was on leave, and his deputy would not sanction the removal of the pilot.

26th June, 1962.

For a full account of a superb run made by driver Donald Beale and fireman Peter Smith with a 9F, unassisted, on the down "Pines" – when they had Baron Vuillet with them on the footplate – see pages 63–66 in Peter Smith's book, "The Somerset & Dorset from the Footplate".

195. B.R. class 4 4-6-0 No. 75073 (one of Bath M.P.D.'s double-chimney class 4s) and S.R. Pacific No. 34043 "Combe Martin", emerge from Devonshire Tunnel and coast down the 1 in 50 bank into Bath with the 12.20 p.m. (SO) Bournemouth to Nottingham.

14th July, 1962.

196. The down "Pines Express" standing at Evercreech Junction, where B.R. class 4 No. 75023 (a Templecombe M.P.D. single-chimney class 4) has just come off after piloting S.R. Pacific No. 34042 "Dorchester" over the Mendips with the "Pines". Whilst the Pacific took water, 75023 has uncoupled and drawn forward before setting back on to the up line to leave the road clear for the express to continue its journey south. The engineman on the left is driver Ray Stokes who was in charge of 75023.

14th April, 1962.

197. A 'bird's-eye' view of Bath Motive Power Depot. In the foreground is the old S&D shed which was largely made of wood, had four roads and could hold 18 engines. The roof of the much smaller, stone-built ex-Midland shed can just be seen above the top of tbe brick-built coaling stage which had been put up in 1953/4 to replace the original wooden structure, built in 1884.

14th July, 1962.

198. Two London Midland Region engines, 5XP class 4-6-0 No. 45739, "Ulster" and Horwich 'Crab' 2-6-0 No. 42827, waiting to take over – for the continuation of the run north – trains coming up from Bournemouth on the S&D.

1st September, 1962.

BATH SHED'S FINAL YEAR OF FEVERISH ACTIVITY ON SUMMER SATURDAYS

BATH MOTIVE POWER DEPOT

199. A Line-up of locomotives outside the S&D shed – S&D 7F 2-8-0 No.53807, B.R. 9F 2-10-0 No. 92245, B.R. class 4 4-6-0 No. 75073 and – complete with 'Pines Express' headboard – 9F 2-10-0 No. 92220 "Evening Star".

8th September, 1962.

200. Three engines pose outside the small, stone-built, ex-Midland shed – which could only be reached via the turntable in the foreground. The three are – ex S&D 4F 0-6-0 No. 44558, B.R. class 3MT 2-6-2T. No. 82041 and ex-L.M.S. 4F 0-6-0 No. 44146.

26th August, 1962.

201. S&D 7F No. 53810 passes Masbury Up Distant signal as she plods steadily uphill with the 1.50 p.m. goods from Evercreech Junction up to Bath.

26th June, 1962.

THE S&D 7F 2-8-0s ON THEIR NORMAL DUTIES

202.

On a miserable, dull day in early October, 7F No. 53809, after taking water at Shepton Mallet, sets off again on the continuation of the steep descent down the southern slopes of the Mendips with the 8.55 a.m. Bath to Evercreech Junction goods.

6th October, 1962.

This is the 7F which was saved from the scrapyard by Mr. Frank Beaumont. She has been expertly restored to running order and, kept in immaculate condition, may now be seen at the headquarters of the Midland Railway Trust at Butterley, near Derby.

203. In addition to their normal freight duties, the S&D 7Fs were invariably entrusted with the haulage of pigeon specials which passed over the S&D. This pigeon special from Crewe – seen here nearing Binegar – had been taken over at Bath by 7F No. 53806 for the run over the S&D down to Templecombe where the birds were to be released for their flight home.

19th May, 1962.

204.
Although it appears not to have been widely known amongst the railway enthusiast fraternity, the S&D 7F 2-8-0s quite frequently were rostered for hauling freight trains up the Midland line to Westerleigh Yard, north of Mangotsfield. Sometimes they went even further afield and had the occasional run down to Avonmouth. In this picture, S&D 7F No. 53806 is pulling out of the Midland Yard at Bath with a freight bound for Westerleigh.

28th April, 1962.

THE FIVE SURVIVING S&D 7F 2-8-0s ON PASSENGER SERVICE

205.

7F No. 53806 coming up the final few yards to Masbury Summit with the 7.35 a.m. (SO) Nottingham to Bournemouth.

11th August, 1962.

206.

The 6.43 a.m. relief from Birmingham to Bournemouth passing through Midsomer Norton, hauled by 7F No. 53807.

28th July, 1962.

207.

7F No. 53809 threads the sand cutting above Broadstone in charge of the 7.35 a.m. (SO) Nottingham to Bournemouth.

25th August, 1962.

208. B.R. class 5 No. 73047, in charge of the 9.25 a.m. (SO) Bournemouth to Manchester and Liverpool, is assisted in the climb over the Mendips by S&D 7F No. 53808. In this picture they are passing through Shepton Mallet. I have no record as to whether the 7F came off at Binegar, or carried on as pilot the whole way through to Bath.
1st September, 1962.

209. S&D 7F 2-8-0 No. 53810, in charge of the 'Up Mail', climbing vigorously up the long stretch of 1 in 50 north of Evercreech New. Because of the fast running required, the 7Fs were not normally rostered to work this train.
11th August, 1962.

210. After the special had arrived back at Evercreech Junction from the run over the branch, 7F No. 53808 again takes charge of the train and sets off from the Junction on the continuation of the run up to Bath.
30th September, 1962.

ENTHUSIASTS' SPECIAL

On Sunday, 30th September, the Locomotive Club of Great Britain ran a special, "The Somerset and Dorset Rail Tour", over the S&D system. 7F No. 53808 was in charge of the train for the run over the main line from Broadstone up to Bath, whilst an ex-G.W.R. 0-6-0 was used to work the special up the branch from Evercreech Junction to Highbridge and back. (See pictures 231 and 232).

211. No. 53808 coming vigorously up the 1 in 50 towards Winsor Hill Tunnel with the special during the course of the 8½-mile climb from Evercreech Junction up to Masbury Summit, 811 feet above sea level.

30th September, 1962.

212. On arrival at Bath another ex-S&D engine, 4F 0-6-0 No. 44558, took over the special and is seen here setting off past Bath Station Box for the run over the Midland line to Bristol, Temple Meads. From Bristol, the train was worked back to London by an ex-G.W.R. '47XX' class 2-8-0. *30th September, 1962.*

213. August – nearing Midford viaduct.
2nd August. 1962.

S&D 4F 0-6-0 No. 44560

For several months this 4F – old No. 60 built for the S&D. J.R. by Armstrong Whitworth & Co. in 1922 – appeared to be Templecombe Shed's favourite engine for use on the 4.15 p.m. up local from Templecombe to Bath.

214.
May - emerging from Combe Down Tunnel into Lyncombe Vale.
17th May, 1962.

215. April – passing over Cole viaduct.

14th April, 1962.

216. – And on a Sunday in September, 44560 was hard at work, in charge of an engineers' train at Evercreech Junction.

30th September, 1962.

BANK HOLIDAY EXCURSIONS

– in 1962 excursions to Bournemouth over the S&D were still as popular as ever.

217. Easter Monday – B.R. class 4 2-6-0 No. 76019 and class 5 No. 73054 running through the reverse curves south of Midford with an excursion from Weston-super-Mare down to Bournemouth.

23rd April, 1962.

218. August, Bank Holiday. – 9F No. 92001 climbing past Moorewood in charge of the 8.50 a.m. excursion from Bristol to Bournemouth.

6th August, 1962.

'THE UP MAIL'

– This train left Bournemouth at 3.40 p.m. every afternoon except Sundays.

This was the most important train to run over the S&D. It carried the mails from the South up to Mangotsfield, on the Midland main line from Bristol, where the mails were transferred to the Evening Mail from Bristol to the North. This connection had to be made. Punctuality was essential and over the S&D, the 3.40 p.m. up had priority over all other traffic – including the down "Pines"! – and was always given the straight run through on all the single line sections.

219. With all Up signals off, the 3.40 p.m. from Bournemouth, hauled by B.R. class 5 No. 73049, approaches Midford and the single line section into Bath Junction.

14th July, 1962.

220. 9F No. 92220 "Evening Star", in charge of the 'Up Mail', crosses over Charlton Road viaduct, Shepton Mallet, and starts on the final 3-mile climb up to Masbury Summit.

12th September, 1962.

221.

Blossom time on the S&D. The 3.20 p.m. Bath to Templecombe stopping train drifts down towards Masbury Halt behind class 4 No. 75009. This was a Templecombe engine – all the standard class 4 4-6-0s shedded at Templecombe had single chimneys.

2nd June, 1962.

THE SOMERSET AND DORSET'S B.R. STANDARD CLASS 4 4-6-0s

With the S&D's increased allocation of these engines, they were now working most of the local services over the main line.

222. No. 75072 – a Bath shed class 4 recently converted to a double blast-pipe and chimney – emerges from Chilcompton Tunnel with the 4.37 p.m. down local from Bath to Templecombe.

14th July, 1962.

223.
Ex-G.W.R. 0-6-0 No. 3206 passes by Shepton Montague with the one-van afternoon perishables from Highbridge to Templecombe. In the days before the Western Region gained control of the S&D, there used to be a regular afternoon milk train from Bason Bridge to Templecombe, – but the W.R. had now diverted this traffic to run up their own line from Highbridge.
7th July, 1962.

THE EX-G.W.R. '2251' CLASS 0-6-0s

By 1962, the Highbridge to Templecombe traffic was mainly in the hands of these ex-G.W.R. 0-6-0s.

224. The 2.20 p.m. local from Highbridge to Templecombe sets off from Evercreech Junction hauled by ex-G.W.R. 0-6-0 No. 3216.
24th February, 1962.

THE B.R. STANDARD CLASS 4 2-6-0s

No engine of this class was ever allocated to an S&D shed, but since 1955 they had run regularly over the line, working originally from Eastleigh shed, and latterly from Bournemouth Central shed.

225. No. 76009, helping out on a busy summer Saturday, climbs towards Masbury with a relief from Bournemouth to Kidsgrove (12 noon off Bournemouth West).

11th August, 1962.

226. The 9.03 a.m. Bristol to Bournemouth (9.55 a.m. off Bath) sets off from Shepton Mallet headed by class 4 No. 76015 and 9F No. 92220 "Evening Star". 76015 was working down to Evercreech Junction to assist an up train over the Mendips, and, as was common practice, had been coupled ahead of the 9.55 a.m. down train engine to save having to find a separate light engine path for her.

1st September, 1962.

227.

No. 76026, in charge of the 1.08 p.m. (SO) Bournemouth to Bristol, coming up to the sand cutting at the summit of the 1 in 97 climb northwards from Broadstone on the 3-mile single line section to Corfe Mullen.

25th August, 1962.

BOURNEMOUTH'S STANDARD CLASS 4 2-6-0s WORKING OVER THE SOMERSET AND DORSET

228.

The 1.08 p.m. (SO) Bournemouth to Bristol again, this time hauled by No. 76019, approaching Evercreech New at the start of the 8½-mile climb up the southern slopes of the Mendips.

7th July, 1962.

THE BRANCH

The physical characteristics of the branch, which was single-line and ran west from Evercreech Junction for 22 miles over to Highbridge, could hardly have been more different from those of the S&D's main line north from Evercreech Junction up to Bath. In place of the main line's almost continuous succession of curves, and long, very steep gradients, the branch – apart from the occasional curve and Pylle bank – ran almost as straight as a die for mile after mile and was virtually level.

229. Ex-G.W.R. 0-6-0 No. 2219 prepares to stop at Shapwick in the late afternoon with the 4.00 p.m. local from Highbridge down to Templecombe.
3rd November, 1962.

230.
The 2.20 p.m. Highbridge to Templecombe local, hauled by ex-G.W.R. 0-6-0 No. 3206, standing in West Pennard station. Westwards from West Pennard towards Glastonbury the line ran dead straight for over 4 miles, and in this picture, can be seen stretching away to a pinpoint in the distance.
3rd November, 1962.

ENTHUSIASTS' SPECIAL OVER THE BRANCH

On Sunday, 30th September, the Locomotive Club of Great Britain ran a special "The Somerset and Dorset Rail Tour" over the S&D system. (See pictures 210–212). For the run up the branch from Evercreech Junction to Highbridge and back, the train was hauled by ex-G.W.R. 0-6-0 No. 3210.

231. The special running westwards past Pylle.

30th September, 1962.

232. With fireman George Stent leaning out of the cab to make sure the line was clear of small boys, 3210 sets off from Glastonbury for the continuation of the run west over to Highbridge. Glastonbury Tor can be seen in the distance, just in front of the engine's smoke box.

30th September, 1962.

A FOOTPLATE RUN ON A 4F-HAULED GOODS UP THE BRANCH

One misty morning in October, I had the great good fortune of being invited by my friend Mr. Harold Morris, the Bath shed-master – whose appointment also covered Highbridge – to accompany him on a footplate run over the branch on the morning goods from Evercreech Junction.

233. Mr. Harold Morris, fireman Leslie Warren and driver George Wheadon standing in front of our engine, 4F No. 44272, before departure from Evercreech Junction Up yard. Walking up on the right is shunter Charlie Vaughan.
23rd October, 1962.

234. Fireman Leslie Warren – whose dinner sandwiches were said to be the largest ever seen on the branch!

235. Mr. Harold Morris and driver George Wheadon.

236. We were held at West Pennard to cross an eastbound goods. Looking forward from the 4F's cab, one could see the single-line stretching ahead for miles, as straight as a die, until it was finally swallowed up in the mist in the far distance.

23rd October, 1962.

237. We returned from Highbridge to Evercreech Junction "on the cushions". The Whitaker mechanical apparatus for the exchange of tablets was not used on the branch, so as we approached Evercreech Junction North Box – and the end of the branch – our fireman held out the single-line token from West Pennard for signalman Bill Harris to take by hand.

MY LAST FOOTPLATE RUN ON "THE PINES EXPRESS"

On Tuesday, 31st July, I was granted the privilege of a footplate permit for the down "Pines Express" from Bath down to Bournemouth. It was to be my last footplate run on the "Pines".

238. The engine for the down "Pines" on 31st July was 9F No. 92233, in the charge of driver Donald Beale and passed fireman Peter Smith, and I was accompanied by locomotive inspector Lawrence Whitley. Just before we moved off shed I took this picture of my friends (from the left) passed fireman Peter Smith, locomotive inspector Lawrence Whitley, driver Donald Beale, and shed-master Harold Morris who had come to see me off and wish me a good run.

31st July, 1962.

239.
On the 16-mile single-line between Templecombe and Blandford Forum, we were held for a while in the loop at Shillingstone, to cross the 3.40 p.m. from Bournemouth, the "Up Mail", seen approaching hauled by sister engine, 9F No. 92210. As already mentioned (see pictures 219 and 220), the "Up Mail" had priority over all other traffic on the S&D.

31st July, 1962.

240. Approaching Broadstone, the end of the 3-mile single-line section from Corfe Mullen – and also the end of the S&D's own track. We were about to run on to Southern track over which we would now travel for the final 8½ miles of our journey into Bournemouth West.
31st July, 1962.

241. (Left) On the descent from Broadstone down to Poole, we met a Southern train coming up the bank, hauled by U class 2-6-0 No. 31619. The track on the right, next to the siding on which the coaches are standing, ran to Hamworthy Junction.
31st July, 1962.

242. My train home – class 5 No. 73047 stands in the early evening at the head of the 6.50 p.m. up for Bath. Alongside, in the adjacent platform is class 4 No. 76008 with a Southern train.
After a most enjoyable run down to Bournemouth, during which Driver Donald Beale and passed fireman Peter Smith had given me a brilliant display of the astounding capabilities of a 9F, the run home was a bit of an anti-climax! With Lawrence Whitley I came home on the 6.50 p.m. from Bournemouth, arriving in Bath, tired but very happy, at 10.21 p.m.
31st July, 1962.

THE LAST "PINES EXPRESS"

The fateful day arrives, Saturday, 8th September, 1962, heralding the last runs over the Somerset and Dorset of "The Pines Express". Both the up train in the morning and the down in the afternoon, were hauled by 9F No. 92220 "Evening Star", unassisted.

243. (Right) On the morning up "Pines", "Evening Star" was driven by passed fireman Peter Smith with Aubrey Punter firing to him. I took this picture of Peter (left) and Aubrey with "Evening Star" on Bath shed at the conclusion of their epic run up from Bournemouth. For a graphic account of their exploits, reference should be made to Peter Smith's book "Mendips Engineman".
8th September, 1962.

244. Peter Smith accelerates "Evening Star" very rapidly away from Cole, where the up "Pines" had been held for over ten minutes due to the preceding train – the 9.25 a.m. from Bournemouth West – grossly exceeding the booked time for her stop at Evercreech Junction.
Apparently, on arrival at the junction, the driver of the 9.25 a.m., which was 9F hauled, said he had not enough coal for the run up to Bath, and requested assistance. But as this train was booked for a 9F, no pilot engine was waiting at the junction to assist over the Mendips. However, an ex-G.W.R. Collett 0-6-0 was shunting the Up yard, and this was hastily summoned and came backing down to the station to couple on to the 9F. But the 9F's driver said he was not happy about having a comparatively light 0-6-0 coupled ahead of his heavy 2-10-0, and insisted on the engines changing places, with the Collett being coupled inside, next to the train.
Whilst all this palaver was going on at the junction, the up "Pines Express" was being held at Cole – with Peter Smith 'champing at the bit' and "Evening Star" beginning to blow off furiously. The ever lengthening delay must have been most disappointing for Peter Smith and his fireman Aubrey Punter, for they had set their hearts on a 'right time' arrival at Bath with the last up "Pines", and this would now be an impossibility.
8th September, 1962.

245. With the battle won, "Evening Star" comes triumphantly up to Masbury Summit with the up "Pines Express". At 426 tons, this was the heaviest train ever taken over the Mendips, unassisted. No wonder Aubrey Punter is looking a bit exhausted as he leans out of the 9F's cab as he must have had a lot of very hard work to do over the preceding 8½ miles.

8th September, 1962.

246. – And finally, breasting the summit at Masbury, 811 feet above sea level, at the end of the 8½ mile climb, much of it at 1 in 50, up the southern slopes of the Mendips from Evercreech Junction.

8th September, 1962.

247. The down "Pines Express" comes thundering up through Midsomer Norton hauled by "Evening Star". The crew for the down run in the afternoon was driver Peter Guy and fireman Ronald Hyde, and their expert handling of the 9F resulted in another splendid run.
8th September, 1962.

THE LAST DOWN "PINES"

Just as I was finishing this book, I had a fascinating and amusing letter from Mr. David Walder who, in 1962, was Assistant to the District Locomotive Superintendent, and rode with the crew on "Evening Star" on the last down "Pines" from Bath as far as Evercreech Junction. I quote from his letter –

"The Branksome men were keen to make a record trip, and I was obliged officially to dissuade them from collecting an empty coach to add to what was already a full load. The start from Green Park was explosive in two senses – the mass of detonators, and the vigorous driving. The rate of temperature build-up in the fire box was such that when we wished to fire, approaching Combe Down Tunnel, the firehole doors had jammed and the coalpick as well as the hose had to be used to slide the doors open.

You will perhaps remember that as the train climbed towards Binegar the exhaust was fairly sharp! (See picture 248 on opposite page). We could I think have stopped at Evercreech Junction in a slightly better time than that achieved earlier the same summer, when Baron Vuillet had such a remarkable run, had it not been for a signal check on our way down the bank – perhaps operating doubled our intention to stop at the junction".

248. "Evening Star" climbing very rapidly up the 1 in 70 towards Binegar with the last down "Pines". David Walder, wearing felt hat, and fireman Ronald Hyde, can be seen looking out from the 9F's cab.

8th September, 1962.

249. The Sad Farewell. As "Evening Star" passed through Cole with the last down "Pines Express", it was seen that, during the stop at Evercreech Junction, someone had hung a pine wreath on her smokebox door.

8th September, 1962.

250. As 1962 drew to a close, the light at the end of the Somerset and Dorset's tunnel was already beginning to fade. Less than 4 years later it would have gone for ever.

The Somerset and Dorset in the 'Sixties

PART 4
1963~1966

THE SOMERSET AND DORSET IN DEEPEST WINTER

Whilst the snow lay round about, deep and crisp and even, 7F No. 53808 plodded slowly away up the 1 in 60 southwards from Midford with the 11.00a.m. down goods from Bath.
15th January, 1963.

THE AUTUMN OF THE SOMERSET AND DORSET

By late September 1965, it was already known that the Somerset and Dorset had not much longer to live. The Standard 2-6-4 tanks had only appeared on the S&D near the end of the line's existence, but these most competent locomotives proved a boon to the Somerset and Dorset in its final years. In this scene, 2-6-4T No. 80041 is nearing Wellow with the 4.15p.m. up train from Templecombe in the early evening of a lovely autumn day.

29th September, 1965.

The Somerset and Dorset in the 'Sixties

PART 4
1963 ~ 1966

by
Ivo Peters B.E.M.

ON THE BRANCH

S&D 4F No. 44560, in charge of an enthusiasts' special, draws near to Glastonbury.

28th March, 1965.

INTRODUCTION

This is the last book of a four part series covering the Somerset and Dorset Railway in the Fifties and Sixties. Volume 3 covered the period from the beginning of 1960 to the end of 1962. This volume now takes us from 1963 to the sad end of the line, in March 1966.

To all intents and purposes, the fate of the Somerset and Dorset had been sealed in 1962 when, at the end of the summer service, the "Pines Express" and all other through trains between the Midlands and the North, and Bournemouth, had been diverted away from the S&D to run over other routes. In one deft move, the Somerset and Dorset had been reduced to being little more than a country branch line providing a purely local service and there could now be little reason left to doubt the intentions of the Western Region to close the line. Once this decision had been reached, the sensible step would have been to carry out the execution as quickly as possible. But instead, it appeared that a deliberate policy had been adopted to allow the Somerset and Dorset gradually to decline to a totally uneconomic state, and die a lingering death. A typical example of this policy was the 1963 Timetable which remained virtually unchanged from the busy "Pines" days of 1962. Although the "Pines" no longer ran over the S&D, the local ancillary services to this express, such as the 4.16p.m. down stopping train which started from the remote country spot of Evercreech Junction and used to follow the "Pines" down to Bournemouth, still ran, but now empty, carrying non-existent passengers from a 'ghost' "Pines".

In 1964, all night freight traffic which included the "Down Mail", was withdrawn, and the Somerset and Dorset closed at night. At the same time, the relentless policy continued to be pursued by the Western Region of diverting away from the S&D as much goods traffic as possible until soon only one freight train per day ran between Bath and Evercreech Junction. But then, just when all hope was fading of saving the Somerset and Dorset, salvation suddenly seemed on hand. In October 1964, there was a change of Government, the Socialists replacing the Conservatives. In their manifesto, Labour stated that there would be no more major rail closures until plans for co-ordination of road and rail transport had been drawn up. When Labour won the General Election, the staff of the Somerset and Dorset were elated, for to shut their system of over 85 miles would surely be a major closure and this would not now take place. Alas, they were wrong. After an angonisingly long wait, the Labour Government finally sanctioned the closure of the Somerset and Dorset which took place on 7th March, 1966.

Ivo Peters
1982

THE SOMERSET AND DORSET IN ALL SEASONS

THE HEIGHT OF SUMMER

On a lovely warm June morning, BR Class 5 No. 73051 comes up to Masbury Summit with an excursion from Bath to Bournemouth.

7th June, 1965.

. . . AND THE DEPTH OF WINTER

With the temperature well below freezing, 8F No. 48737 storms through Midford, as she commences the steep climb up to and through Combe Down Tunnel, with the 6.25 a.m. goods from Evercreech Junction.

15th January, 1963.

1. 4F No. 44272 appears round the corner, running downhill through the reverse curves towards Midford with the 12.45 p.m. up local from Templecombe. The very heavy falls of snow had blocked many roads, completely isolating numerous villages from the outside world, except for the lucky few, such as Wellow, which were served by the S&D. In the severe winter of 1981/2, Wellow again became totally 'snowed in'. How many elderly residents must have remembered the dear old S&D and wished that it was still in existence?

10th January, 1963.

1963

THE SOMERSET AND DORSET IN DEEPEST WINTER

Towards the end of December, 1962, it started to snow and as the New Year came in, some of the worst blizzards in living memory swept the south-west of England. High up on the Mendips, conditions grew steadily worse until on Thursday, 3rd January, the Somerset and Dorset was finally overwhelmed; blocked completely by massive drifts. The staff of the S&D made tremendous efforts to re-open their line, but it was not until three days later, on Sunday, 6th January, that one line was eventually cleared between Binegar and Shepton Mallet, allowing single line working to be initiated over this section. Even after the line had been re-opened, Somerset lay under a heavy blanket of snow for several weeks and it was not until late February that it was possible to get back to normal working.

When summer eventually came to the Somerset and Dorset, it bore no resemblance to previous years, for at the end of the 1962 summer service, the "Pines Express" and all other through trains between the Midlands and the North, and Bournemouth, had been re-routed away from the S&D. The line was now reduced to providing a purely local service and heavy double-headed trains, once an everyday sight, were now a rarity.

Changes were also taking place on the locomotive side. Another of the S&D Armstrong 4Fs, No. 44559, had been withdrawn, and Bath Motive Power Depot was receiving Stanier 8F 2-8-0s as replacements for the 1914 series S&D 7Fs, the last of which had been withdrawn in 1962. All five of the later 1925 series, however, were still in service, although the first of these, No. 53810, was to be withdrawn in December.

In July, due to the non-availability of so many engines, Bath Depot asked for the loan of two BR Standard Class 5 locomotives. These were not forthcoming, but instead two Class 9Fs, Nos. 92224 and 92220 "Evening Star" arrived on temporary transfer. However, their stay on the S&D was short, for with no steam-heating facilities, they could not be used on passenger trains after the end of September.

Finally, in November, a type which had not previously appeared on the S&D scene, the BR Standard Class 4 2-6-4 tank, started to work over the line. They were not, however, introduced by the Western Region but by the Southern Region. Bournemouth Motive Power Depot was responsible for providing the power for the 1.10 p.m. up, Bournemouth West to Bath (7.05 p.m. return ex-Bath) and decided to try out one of these engines on this turn. The test proved most successful and from then on, increasing numbers of these engines were used on the S&D right up to the end of the line in 1966.

2. No. 53810, the last of the batch of five 7F 2-8-0s built by Robert Stephenson & Co., in 1925, for the Somerset and Dorset, coasts down past Norton Hill Colliery with the 6.05a.m. up goods from Templecombe. No. 53810 was condemned in December 1963, and so became the first of the 1925 series S&D 7Fs to be withdrawn from service.

27th September, 1963.

TWO LOCOMOTIVE 'EVENTS' OF 1963 –

The first withdrawal from service of one of the 1925 series S&D 7Fs and the surprising and, in some ways, rather pathetic, return of "Evening Star" to the S&D.

3. "Evening Star" standing in Evercreech Junction Station with the 3 coach 1.10p.m. down stopping train.

12th September, 1963.

At the conclusion of the 1962 summer service, the "Pines Express" and all other through trains, had been re-routed away from the Somerset and Dorset, so reducing the line to one operating a purely local service between Bath and Bournemouth.

In 1962, "Evening Star" had been sent, on short term loan, to Bath Shed to work the last "Pines Express" to run over the S&D. But when, in the summer of 1963, she was again transferred to Bath, Green Park Depot, the appearance of this immensely powerful 2-10-0 on the Somerset and Dorset, caused considerable surprise. With no heavy passenger trains still running over the line and being unsuitable for freight work because her length prevented her from being turned at either Evercreech Junction or Templecombe, "Evening Star" spent her days on the S&D ambling between Bath and Bournemouth with featherweight stopping trains of three or four coaches.

4. S&D 7F No. 53809 stands just north of Binegar with the brake van and the last four wagons of the previous Thursday's 3.30a.m. down goods. No. 53809, and her sister engine No. 53807, had just succeeded in recovering the rear portion of this train from the deep snow-drift near Winsor Hill, where it had lain marooned for the last three days.
6th January, 1963.

5. A view looking back from the plough engine, 'Jinty' No. 47496, at 8F No. 48660 pushing heartily behind, as the two engines forged their way, 'wrong line', uphill in a successful attempt to clear the up line between Midsomer Norton and Binegar. Earlier in the morning they had succeeded, as can be seen, in clearing the down line. Seconds after taking this picture, the back of my head and shoulders was hit by a great wave of snow as we charged into a drift near Moorewood; much to the amusement of the crew of the 8F who had seen what was coming!
6th January, 1963.

THE SOMERSET AND DORSET IS OVERWHELMED BY SNOW

Late on the evening of Wednesday, 2nd January, it began snowing heavily, whereupon pre-arranged plans were immediately put into action for the snowplough engine to precede the "Down Mail" in the early hours of the following morning. At 2.20a.m. on the Thursday morning, 3rd January, the snowplough engine, a 'Jinty' tank driven by Doug Holden with Graham Tughill as his fireman, set off from Bath, 20 minutes ahead of the 2.40a.m. "Down Mail", which was in the charge of Driver Harold Burford, Fireman Edward Paulley and Guard William Parratt. After a tremendous battle climbing the northern slopes of the Mendips, the two crews fought their way over Masbury Summit, only to become trapped in a massive drift south of Shepton Mallet.

After hours of ceaseless effort, both crews at last succeeded in digging out their engines and managed to get them down to Evercreech Junction to replenish their water supplies. They then struggled back uphill to the "Mail", only to find that all their efforts had been in vain, for the situation was now hopeless with the train buried deep in the snow.

Meanwhile, unaware of the drama taking place down the line, two more trains, the 3.30a.m. and 5.00a.m. down goods had both set off from Bath. The 3.30a.m. was manned by Driver Fred Love, Fireman Tony Pitt and Guard Frederick Nowell, whilst the 5.00a.m. was in the charge of Driver Sidney Carter, Fireman Colin Powis and Guard Roy Hayward.

With a full blizzard now raging, their experiences were even more traumatic than those of their colleagues with the "Down Mail". Both trains became completely overwhelmed by gigantic drifts; the 3.30a.m. near Winsor Hill and the 5.00a.m. close to Binegar. Guard Fred Nowell heroically struggled for hours through the snow down to Shepton Mallet, to report the situation concerning his train, whilst Fred Love and Tony Pitt, after throwing out their engine's fire, managed to reach a nearby farmhouse, where they were taken in by the farmer and his wife, and after 'thawing out', were treated to an enormous breakfast of eggs and bacon.

For three days the Somerset and Dorset remained closed, completely overwhelmed by snow on the high Mendips and it was not until the Sunday, 6th January, that the 3.30a.m. down goods, 'lost' since the previous Thursday, was finally dug out and the rear portion hauled back up to Binegar by two S&D 7Fs. In the meantime, three engines had managed to battle their way up from the south and retrieve the engine and front part of the train which they took down to Evercreech Junction.

With one line now successfully cleared over Masbury Summit, single line working became possible between Binegar and Shepton Mallet and the S&D was open again.

For the train crews who fought so valiantly against impossible odds, trying to get through to their destination, and for the many members of the S&D staff who toiled ceaselessly for long hours in appalling conditions to re-open their line, no praise is too high.

6. At Binegar the snow had almost reached up to platform level in the station. Much of this had to be dug out the hard way, by hand, before it was safe for the plough engine and her assisting 8F to pass through on their way to tackle the clearance of the up line between Binegar and Shepton Mallet. To have attempted to 'charge' the deep snow trapped between the platforms would have courted disaster, for the platforms would have prevented the snow from being thrown clear. Had the snow built up between the platform face and the side of the plough engine, it could easily have led to her derailment.

6th January, 1963.

BINEGAR

7.

The plough engine, 'Jinty' No. 47496, and her assisting 8F No. 48660, stand at the north end of Binegar Station after successfully clearing the up line between Midsomer Norton and Binegar. As described in the caption to picture 6 above they were waiting for the level of snow to be reduced between the platforms before setting off to endeavour to clear the up line between Binegar and Shepton Mallet.

6th January, 1963.

8.

The plough engine and her assisting 8F are about to set off from Midsomer Norton, 'wrong line', in an attempt to clear the up line between Midsomer Norton and Binegar.

6th January, 1963.

MIDSOMER NORTON

9.

8F No. 48660; the same 8F which, two days earlier, had played such an important part in assisting the 'Jinty' plough engine to clear the line, comes plodding steadily up the 1 in 50 towards Midsomer Norton with the 2.00 p.m. down goods from Bath. After her weekend's exertions, it seemed only poetic justice that she was receiving maximum help in the rear from one of Radstock's 'Jintys'.

8th January, 1963.

MIDFORD

10.

(Right) 7F No. 53808 running tender first, approaches Midford with a special up coal train from Writhlington Colliery.

26th January, 1963.

11.

(Below) On a dull morning in early January, shortly before it started to snow again, No. 53808 appeared, drifting slowly round the curve, near Lower Twinhoe, with the 10.40 a.m. up coal train from Norton Hill Colliery. Midford up distant signal had been 'on' and, as anticipated by her crew, No. 53808 was brought to a stand at Midford's up outer home signal, as a down train was occupying the single line section between Bath Junction and Midford.

8th January, 1963.

These two pictures figure S&D 2-8-0 No. 53808, the 7F which has been preserved by the Somerset and Dorset Railway Trust and is being restored to running order at the Trust's headquarters at Washford on the West Somerset Railway.

THE MIDFORD VALLEY

Somerset and Dorset scenery, often breathtaking in summer, could be savage in winter.

12.

Brrr!! It must have been bitterly cold on the footplate of S&D 4F No. 44558, running tender first, as she struggled up the steep stretch of 1 in 60 south of Midford with a long train of empty wagons for the collieries around Radstock. Shortly after passing me, the 4F suddenly slipped violently and, although her driver quickly had her under control again, she was not far from stalling!

23rd January, 1963.

13.

In sharp contrast, BR Class 5 No. 73054, in charge of the 9.55a.m. down semi-fast from Bath to Bournemouth, and with only three coaches and a van on, came sailing past me in fine style as she climbed southwards away from Midford.

23rd January, 1963.

14.

4F No. 43853 comes across Midford Viaduct with the 5.05 a.m. up goods from Templecombe, gathering all the speed she can for the coming attack on the steep climb up to, and through, Combe Down Tunnel.

23rd January, 1963.

15.

(Below) After her brief stop at Midford, BR Class 4 4-6-0 No. 75071 pulls away across the viaduct on the continuation of her run south from Bath to Templecombe with the 3.20 p.m. down local.

26th January, 1963.

16. 8F No. 48468 passes the grounds of Midford Castle as she climbs towards Combe Down Tunnel with the 6.25 a.m. up goods from Evercreech Junction.

25th September, 1963.

THE S&D's Ex-LMS STANIER 8F 2-8-0s

With the stud of S&D 7Fs now down to five locomotives, and soon sadly to be reduced to four, ex-LMS 8Fs were appearing in increasing numbers on the Somerset and Dorset.

Although freight engines like the S&D 7Fs, the Stanier 8Fs were versatile locomotives and this led to their occasional use on passenger trains. Unfortunately, also like the S&D 2-8-0s, they were not fitted with steam heating facilities and so could not be used on passenger work after the end of September. However, amongst the 8Fs allocated to the S&D there was one exception, No. 48309. Together with sister engine No. 48728, No. 48309 had been specially fitted with steam heating facilities some years earlier when being prepared for hauling the "Royal Train" through mid-Wales.

17. (Below) At the same location again, 8F No. 48737 coasts down towards Midford with the 8.15 a.m. down local from Bath to Templecombe.

28th September, 1963.

THE BR STANDARD CLASS 4 2-6-4 TANKS START RUNNING OVER THE SOMERSET AND DORSET

Introduced at the 'eleventh hour', (the first appearance of a BR Standard Class 4 2-6-4 tank on the S&D scene was on 4th November 1963), these engines worked in increasing numbers over the Somerset and Dorset and served the line well in its dying days.

18.

In the late afternoon, shortly before sunset, No. 80081 takes water at Evercreech Junction whilst in charge of an up train from Bournemouth. With dusk drawing near, the fireman is taking the opportunity of lighting the engine's lamps.

23rd November, 1963.

19. (Below) No. 80081 again, this time setting off from Shillingstone, on a bright but cold winter's afternoon, with the 1.10 p.m. up stopping train from Bournemouth to Bath.

28th December, 1963.

ONE OF THE S&D's CLASS 5s, No. 73049 RECEIVES A GENERAL OVERHAUL AT EASTLEIGH

This included being repainted in fully lined out green livery.

BEFORE

20. No. 73049 stands in the middle road at Evercreech Junction and looks decidedly woebegone. At some time or another a small 'contretemps' had caused a slight buckling of her right hand running plate.

20th April, 1963.

AFTER

21. Just back from Eastleigh, and resplendent in her new livery of fresh green paint, fully lined out, No. 73049 drifts down to Midford with the 9.55a.m. down semi-fast from Bath to Bournemouth.

5th October, 1963.

THE UNEXPECTED RETURN OF 9F 2-10-0s TO THE SOMERSET AND DORSET

At the beginning of August, due to several locomotives being away at the same time under repair, Bath Motive Power Depot became temporarily embarrassed for power and asked for the loan of two Class 5 locomotives. These were not forthcoming, but instead two 9F 2-10-0s were sent to Bath Shed. The first to arrive was No. 92224, followed shortly by No. 92220 "Evening Star". The 9Fs' arrival caused some resentment because they were much too powerful, and therefore unnecessarily heavy on coal, for the 3 and 4 coach trains now being worked over the S&D. An added complication was that they could only be used between Bath and Bournemouth as their length precluded them from being turned on the turntable near Evercreech Junction North Box, which effectively eliminated their use on freight work.

22. No. 92220 "Evening Star" emerges from Chilcompton Tunnel with the 3 coach 1.10 p.m. down stopping train from Bath.

7th September, 1963.

23. No. 92224 stands in Shepton Mallet Station at the head of the 3.40 p.m. from Bournemouth: the "Up Mail".

7th September, 1963.

FERTILIZER SPECIAL

For many years regular trains of fertilizer had been run from Avonmouth down to Blandford Forum via the S&D, but this train was to be one of the last. The Western Region now re-routed this traffic to run via Bristol, Bath Spa, Westbury, Salisbury, Southampton and Bournemouth; a journey of 135 miles instead of the 65 miles over the S&D, solely to deprive the Somerset and Dorset line of this traffic!

24. S&D 7F No. 53806 climbs past Midsomer Norton with her twenty vans of fertilizer.
4th May, 1963.

25. Drawing near to Moorewood. A 'Jinty' tank is banking vigorously at the rear.
4th May, 1963.

26. Coming up to Masbury Summit, 811 feet above sea level, and the end of the 7½ mile climb from Radstock up the northern slopes of the Mendips. The banker is getting ready to drop off and then return downhill 'wrong line' to Binegar.

4th May, 1963.

BANKING FROM RADSTOCK UP TO MASBURY SUMMIT

As the year progressed, freight carried by the S&D continued to fall as the Western Region diverted more and more traffic away from the line. Apart from coal traffic from the Radstock/Midsomer Norton area, which ran mostly into Bath, southbound goods traffic over the S&D was declining rapidly, and a banked goods from Radstock up to Masbury Summit, once so common, was now becoming a rare sight.

27. The usual practice for bankers, returning light engine from Masbury Summit down to Radstock, was to stop at Chilcompton to take water. In this picture, No. 47557 has just had her tanks topped up, and posing proudly for me in front of their 'Jinty' are Driver Charlie Rawlings and Fireman Eric Wilson. Standing on the engine's running plate is Peter Harding, a Radstock porter, who had been up at Chilcompton filling the signal lamps and was about to have a lift back down to Radstock on the 'Jinty'.

1st November, 1963.

28. 8F No. 48330 runs into Bath from the north with an 18 bogie pigeon special.

17th August, 1963.

PIGEON SPECIAL

On Saturday, 17th August, 8F No. 48330 arrived at Bath with an 18 bogie pigeon special. At Bath, nine vans were taken off and the birds were released. Another 8F, No. 48737 then took the remaining nine bogies on down to Templecombe from where the rest of the birds were released for their flight home.

29. Bath 8F, No. 48737 is about to set off from Green Park with the nine vans for Templecombe.

17th August, 1963.

30. Heading south from Midford. Note that by this time the short siding off the up line had been lifted and the small hut housing the ground frame had been removed.

17th August, 1963.

31.

The 8Fs were too long to be turned on the turntable at Templecombe. So, Saturday, 17th August being a lovely day, the crew of No. 48737 decided to stop at Evercreech Junction North, turn their engine on the turntable there, and then continue the run down to Templecombe, tender first. Their engine was now facing the right direction for the run back up to Bath, in the evening, with the empty vans. Having turned their engine on the turntable at Evercreech Junction North, they are seen here heading south, tender first, through Cole.

17th August, 1963.

32. No. 53808, the 7F preserved by the Somerset and Dorset Railway Trust, nears Bitton with a northbound goods from Bath, Green Park, up to Westerleigh.

2nd March, 1963.

S&D 7Fs 'AWAY FROM HOME'

The Western Region's policy of diverting freight away from the S&D, often made the 7Fs available for use on the Midland line north from Bath.

33. On a warm June evening, S&D 7F No. 53807 passes Kelston Woods with the 6.25 p.m. Bath, Green Park, to Avonmouth fre

ON THE BRANCH –

EASTBOUND PASSENGER TRAINS AT WEST PENNARD

With much of the passenger service over the branch worked by Collett 0-6-0s, the ex-GWR influence was felt far more on the branch than on the main line.

34. The 2.20 p.m. stopping train from Highbridge, departs behind ex-GWR 0-6-0 No. 2219.
21st September, 1963.

35.

Two weeks earlier, the 2.20 p.m. from Highbridge was in the hands of an ex-GWR 0-6-0 No. 3210, seen here setting off for Evercreech Junction.
7th September, 1963.

BATH MOTIVE POWER DEPOT

36. 9F 2-10-0 No. 92224 stands on Bath's 60ft. turntable, which she was just able to do! The 9Fs had a wheelbase of 55ft. 11in. and an overall length of 66ft. 2in.

14th September, 1963.

37.

A picture with a tinge of sadness. Mr. Harold Morris, the popular Bath Shedmaster, says 'au revoir' to Driver Charlie Rawlings, the genial and well-known Radstock driver, who was just coming up to retirement.

2nd November, 1963.

38.

'Jinty' 0-6-0T No. 47544 stands inside the entrance to the old Midland shed.

12th October, 1963.

39. By 1963, boiler wash-outs were no longer carried out at Radstock, so once a fortnight, a Radstock crew would bring one of their 'Jintys' over to Bath for a boiler wash-out, and then return to Radstock with another 'Jinty' which had been serviced and made ready for them. In this picture, No. 47496 has just been brought over to Bath by Driver Charlie Rawlings, whilst sister engine No. 47544 is ready waiting for him to take back to Radstock. The enginemen lined up alongside No. 47496 are (left to right) Fireman Mike Lodder, Drivers Charlie Rawlings and Fred Beard and Fireman Eric Wilson.

2nd November, 1963.

40.

A view from inside the S&D shed showing the timber-trussed roof. On the right is one of Bath's BR Class 4 4-6-0s No. 75071. An old Bath driver, on being asked if there was not a risk of the timber roof catching fire, made the delightful reply, "Oh yes, it did catch fire quite often, but we always managed to put it out."

4th May, 1963

41. 9F 2-10-0 No. 92220 "Evening Star" stands in the station at the head of a train for Bournemouth West.

12th September, 1963.

BATH, GREEN PARK, STATION

42. 9F 2-10-0 No. 92224 sets off for Templecombe with the 1.10 p.m. down stopping train from Bath. Later in the day, the engine on this diagram ran light engine to Evercreech Junction and then worked the 4.13 p.m. down to Bournemouth West. In the case of the 9F, this entailed running back to Evercreech Junction, tender first.

24th August, 1963.

43. A sign of the times! BR Class 5 4-6-0 No. 73164 sets off from the south platform with the 9.55a.m. down semi-fast for Bournemouth West. Standing in the north platform, at the head of the 3 coach 10.10a.m. local to Bristol, Temple Meads, is "Peak" type 4 diesel No. D12. This working had recently been taken over by the big diesels as a 'filling in' turn between arriving at Bristol from the north, and their booked return run home with a northbound express.

24th September, 1963.

44.

9F No. 92224 arrives at Bath with the 7.12a.m. from Bournemouth.

14th September, 1963

45. SR rebuilt Pacific No. 34042 "Dorchester" gets under way with the 4 coach 4.21 p.m. down semi-fast from Bath to Bournemouth. When heavy trains were running over the line, the Bulleid Light Pacifics were regular visitors to Bath, but by now, the sight of one on the Somerset and Dorset was becoming increasingly rare. The Southern Region still provided the motive power for some rosters over the S&D but, unlike the Western Region, they considered a Class 4 type locomotive to be adequate power for hauling the 3 and 4 coach trains now running over the line. A Pacific locomotive only appeared on the scene in the event of a Class 4 being unavailable.

12th September, 1963.

BATH DEPARTURES

46. 9F 2-10-0 No. 92224 sets off with the 3 coach 1.10 p.m. down stopping train from Bath. The old coach body, seen on the left outside the Midland shed, was used by Bath enginemen for their Mutual Improvement Classes.

14th September, 1963.

BATH JUNCTION

47. BR Class 5 No. 73012 coming in over Bath Junction with the 9.05a.m. up from Templecombe, is 'paced' by ex-GWR pannier tank No. 3742 which is on shunting duties. Also photographing this scene is my old friend, Norman Lockett.

25th September, 1963.

48.

9F No. 92220 "Evening Star", in charge of the 3 coach 1.10p.m. down stopping train, begins the 1 in 50 climb away from Bath Junction at the start of the 4 mile single line section out to Midford.

12th September, 1963.

**BR CLASS 5 No. 73047
ON THE 3.40p.m. "UP MAIL"
NORTH OF MIDFORD**

49. Climbing past the grounds of Midford Castle on a lovely evening in early August.

9th August, 1963.

50. On a hazy evening at the end of July, the "Up Mail" crosses over Tucking Mill Viaduct in Horsecombe Vale on the climb up towards Combe Down Tunnel.

30th July, 1963.

51. 9F No. 92224 stands in Midford Station at the head of the 7.12a.m. up stopping train from Bournemouth West to Bath, Green Park.

24th August, 1963.

MIDFORD

52. The 4.37p.m. down local from Bath, hauled by BR Class 4 4-6-0 No. 75071, leaves Midford Viaduct and runs on to double track, which would now last for the next 32 miles, down to Templecombe.

11th May, 1963.

53. The 3.40p.m. from Bournemouth, the "Up Mail", hauled by 9F No. 92224, approaches Midford.

12th September, 1963.

SOUTH OF MIDFORD

54. One of the double-chimney BR Class 4 4-6-0s, No. 75072, originally allocated to Bath Depot, but now transferred to Templecombe Shed, sets off briskly from Midford on the continuation of her run south with the 3.20p.m. down local from Bath.

27th April, 1963.

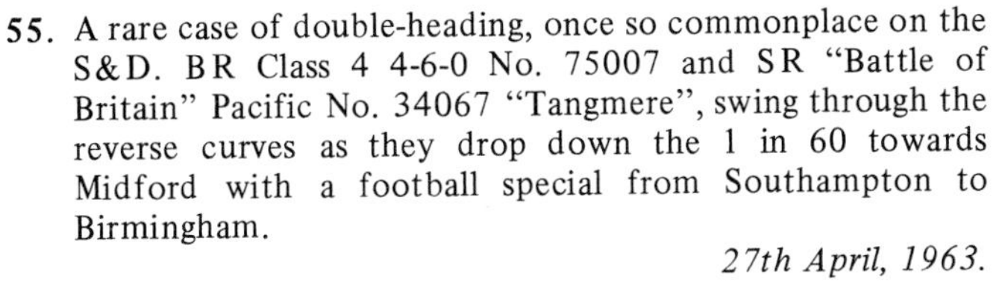

55. A rare case of double-heading, once so commonplace on the S&D. BR Class 4 4-6-0 No. 75007 and SR "Battle of Britain" Pacific No. 34067 "Tangmere", swing through the reverse curves as they drop down the 1 in 60 towards Midford with a football special from Southampton to Birmingham.

27th April, 1963.

56. (Below) Ex-LMS Stanier 8F 2-8-0 No. 48660, in charge of the 1.50 p.m. up goods from Evercreech Junction, is held at Midford's up outer home signal, waiting for the single line section, from Midford into Bath Junction, to become free. Occupying the section at the time was the 4.21 p.m. down from Bath.

25th September, 1963.

WRITHLINGTON

57. 8F No. 48660, hauling the 1.50 p.m. up goods from Evercreech Junction, is shunted on to the down road to let BR Class 4 2-6-0 No. 76015, with the 1.10 p.m. up passenger from Bournemouth West, overtake her. The 1.10 p.m. up from Bournemouth (7.05 p.m. Bath to Bournemouth return) was one of the rosters for which the Southern Region provided the motive power.

25th September, 1963.

SOUTH OF RADSTOCK

58. On a fresh autumn morning in late September, 8F No. 48737, in charge of the 8.15 a.m. down stopping train, has just passed over the Radstock to Midsomer Norton road and is climbing up the 1 in 50 bank towards Midsomer Norton.

28th September, 1963.

59. S&D 7F No. 53807, climbing hard up the long stretch of 1 in 50 with the 8.55 a.m. down goods, draws near to Midsomer Norton.
28th September, 1963.

MIDSOMER NORTON

60.

Partly hidden in the shadow of her own steam, and hauling the 6.05 a.m. up goods from Templecombe, S&D 7F No. 53810 drifts down past Midsomer Norton. On the right, engaged in shunting Norton Hill Colliery yard, is the NCB 0-6-0 saddle tank, "Lord Salisbury", built by Peckett and Sons of Bristol in 1906.
27th September, 1963.

61. BR Standard Class 4 4-6-0 No. 75007, a fairly recent acquisition by Templecombe, but not yet carrying an official shed plate, emerges from Chilcompton Tunnel with the 4.37 p.m. down stopping train from Bath.
14th September, 1963.

CHILCOMPTON TUNNEL

62. The 4.15 p.m. up local from Templecombe coasts down the bank towards the tunnel, hauled by ex-S&D 4F 0-6-0 No. 44560.
14th September, 1963.

CHILCOMPTON

63. Eastleigh Shed's BR Standard Class 4 2-6-0 No. 76006, resumes her journey to Bath with the 1.10p.m. up stopping train from Bournemouth West.

14th September, 1963.

64. Ex-LMS 4F 0-6-0 No. 44422, in charge of the 3.20p.m. down stopping train from Bath, starts to get under way again from Chilcompton Station. Through the platforms the gradient had eased off to 1 in 300, but the 4F was now faced with another long stretch of 1 in 50 in the climb towards Masbury Summit.

14th September, 1963.

65. The 4 coach 4.21 p.m. down semi-
from Bath draws near to Moorew
hauled with nonchalant ease by
2-10-0 No. 92220 "Evening Star".
14th September, 19

MOOREWOOD

66. (Below) In sharp contrast to the
ture above, S&D 7F 2-8-0 No. 53
is having to work hard as she cli
towards Moorewood with
8.55 a.m. down goods from Bath.
7F's crew are Driver Arthur Tur
and Fireman Colin Powis.
28th September, 19

NEAR MASBURY HALT

67. The 3.40 p.m. from Bournemouth, the "Up Mail", passes Masbury Halt up distant signal on the 1 in 50 climb towards Masbury Summit. Most unusually, the train had been made up to six coaches and a van, but this, of course, presented no problem to 9F No. 92220 "Evening Star". Perhaps her crew even appreciated having something a little more worthwhile to haul for a change!
17th August, 1963.

68.

4F 0-6-0 No. 44422 coasts down from the summit towards Masbury Halt with the 3.20 p.m. stopping train from Bath.
14th September, 1963.

69. BR Class 5 No. 73012 prepares to resume her journey to Bournemouth with the 9.55a.m. down semi-fast from Bath. Standing on the right is the 8.55a.m. Bath to Evercreech Junction goods, hauled by S&D 7F No. 53808, which had arrived some twenty minutes earlier. After the 7F had taken water, she set her train back into the siding, situated off the down main line, to leave the road clear for the 9.55a.m. down passenger from Bath.

21st September, 1963.

SHEPTON MALLET

70. (Below) 9F 2-10-0 No. 92224 runs in past the goods shed with the 3.40p.m. from Bournemouth, the "Up Mail", once again made up to six coaches and a van.

7th September, 1963.

71.

Standing in Shepton Mallet Station with the 3 coach 1.10 p.m. down stopping train from Bath, is 9F 2-10-0 No. 92220 "Evening Star".

12th September, 1963.

72.

After dropping down the southern slopes of the Mendips and crossing over Charlton Viaduct, the 3.20 p.m. local from Bath arrives behind S&D 4F 0-6-0 No. 44560.

7th September, 1963.

"EVENING STAR" AT EVERCREECH NEW

73. 9F 2-10-0 "Evening Star" departs from Evercreech New Station with the 7.12a.m. up stopping train from Bournemouth. Ahead now lies the climb up to Shepton Mallet, which includes over three miles of 1 in 50 gradient, but with only three coaches on, this was mere 'child's play' for the 9F. Oh for the days of the up "Pines", with twelve on! Sic transit gloria.
23rd September, 1963.

74. The 3.40p.m. "Up Mail", now composed of the usual three coaches and a van, passes through, hauled by "Evening Star".
13th September, 1963.

EVERCREECH JUNCTION NORTH

75. The 3.20 p.m. down stopping train, hauled by BR Standard Class 4 4-6-0 No. 75073, drifts cautiously round the sharp curve by the North Box. The branch to Highbridge, the original main line of the Somerset Central Railway, can be seen running straight ahead past the box. On the right is one of the distinctive S&D 'calling back' signals. When a down goods arrived from Bath, it came to a stand on the main line, just south of this signal. A shunting engine then coupled on to the rear of the train and it was this 'calling back' signal which authorized the shunting engine driver to draw the train back on the main line and then on to the branch, from where it could be propelled into the up yard.
20th September, 1963.

76.
Ex-LMS Ivatt 2-6-2T No. 41296, sets off with the 5.00 p.m. branch line train for Highbridge. On the left, ex-GWR Collett 0-6-0 No. 3210 is engaged in shunting the up yard.
20th April, 1963.

EVERCREECH JUNCTION

77. BR Standard Class 4 2-6-0 No. 76015, from Bournemouth Central Shed, sets off from Evercreech Junction with the 1.10p.m. up stopping train from Bournemouth West to Bath.

20th April, 1963.

78.

(Below) One of Bath Shed's Stanier 8F 2-8-0s, No. 48468, is pressed into service on passenger work. Her 3 coach train is the 1.10p.m. down local from Bath.

21st September, 1963.

79. The 1.10 p.m. down stopping train again, but on this occasion the three coaches are in the charge of 9F 2-10-0 No. 92220 "Evening Star".
12th September, 1963.

80.

Driver Vic Hunt assists his fireman in getting the bag in for their BR Standard Class 4 2-6-4T No. 80081 to take water. This is the 1.10 p.m. up stopping train from Bournemouth West to Bath, a roster for which the Southern Region provided the motive power. Bournemouth Central Shed (71B) considered a BR Standard Class 4 type locomotive, either a 2-6-0 tender engine or a 2-6-4 tank, to be adequate for working the 3 and 4 coach trains now running over the Somerset and Dorset and they were quickly proved right. From late 1963, the Standard Class 4 2-6-4 tanks played an increasing role in hauling trains over the S&D and they did it very well.
7th December, 1963.

81. BR Class 5 No. 73047 heads north over Cole Viaduct with the 3.40p.m. from Bournemouth: the "Up Mail".

17th August, 1963.

COLE

82. Slowing for her stop at Cole, the 4.15p.m. up local from Templecombe, headed by BR Class 4 4-6-0 No. 75072, appears from under the road bridge at the south end of the station.

17th August, 1963.

83.
The 4.13 p.m. down stopping train, which started from Evercreech Junction, a remote spot in the heart of the countryside, resumes her virtually useless journey, drawn by 4F 0-6-0 No. 44422. In the old days, after the down "Pines" had made her stop at the junction, this local train used to set off directly behind the express, carrying passengers who had travelled down from the north and whose destination was one of the small towns south of Evercreech Junction, where the "Pines" did not stop. Although there was now no longer any "Pines Express", the Western Region having diverted it away from the S&D, the 4.13 p.m. down local still ran, virtually empty, carrying ghost passengers from a non-existent "Pines".

17th August, 1963.

84. BR Class 4 2-6-0 No. 76015 runs in with the 3.20 p.m. down stopping train from Bath.

17th August, 1963.

SHEPTON MONTAGUE

85.

S&D 7F No. 53806 heads south, near Shepton Montague, with one of the last fertilizer specials from Avonmouth to run down the Somerset and Dorset to Blandford Forum *(see pictures 24 to 26)*. The train has just passed beneath the bridge No. 127, known as Rock Cutting Bridge, which carried, over the S&D, a small lane leading from Shepton Montague to the village of Stoke. Compared with other bridges on the S&D, this bridge had a remarkably high clearance, the height from rail level to the soffit of the arch being no less than 21 ft. 2 in.

4th May, 1963.

HORSINGTON

86. The 4.21 p.m. down semi-fast from Bath to Bournemouth, hauled by SR Pacific No. 34103 "Calstock", draws near to Horsington. Bulleid Pacifics were by now becoming quite a rare sight on the S&D and the appearance of "Calstock" was due to the last minute non-availability of the Standard Class 4 locomotive which had been rostered for the turn.

5th August, 1963.

NORTH OF HENSTRIDGE

87. Immaculate power for the "Up Mail". The train, seen here heading north from Henstridge towards Templecombe, is being hauled by BR Standard Class 5 No. 73049, just back from overhaul at Eastleigh Works, which included being finished in fully lined out green livery. *5th October, 1963.*

SHILLINGSTONE

88. The 3.40p.m. from Bournemouth, the "Up Mail", again. This time setting off from Shillingstone behind 9F 2-10-0 No. 92220 "Evening Star".

28th September, 1963.

BLANDFORD FORUM

89. BR Class 5 No. 73047 is seen about to pass through Blandford Forum with an excursion from Bristol to Bournemouth (8.50 a.m. off Bath).

5th August, 1963.

BR STANDARD CLASS 5s ON EXCURSION TRAFFIC TO BOURNEMOUTH ON AUGUST BANK HOLIDAY MONDAY

CORFE MULLEN

90.

The 9.30 a.m. excursion from Bath, hauled by BR Class 5 No. 73054, passes Corfe Mullen. The train has just run on to the start of the 3 mile single line section to Broadstone. The track on the right hand side is the old line to Wimborne which had long been out of use, but a short section was left intact at the Corfe Mullen end to serve Carter's Siding.

5th August, 1963.

91. BR Standard Class 4 4-6-0 No. 75007 climbs the bank with the 12.23 p.m. down from Templecombe.

5th August, 1963.

PARKSTONE BANK

The Somerset and Dorset's own line ended at Broadstone. For the final eight miles of their journey to Bournemouth, S&D trains ran over Southern track. The formidable 1 in 60 Parkstone Bank lay between Poole and Branksome.

92. Two BR Standard Class 4 2-6-0s climb the bank, light engine. It is interesting to compare the two different types of tender fitted to engines of this class.

5th August, 1963.

93. Together for their last meeting. 7F No. 53807, the sole surviving S&D 7F, after her final run down to Evercreech Junction, meets for the last time fellow S&D engine, 4F No. 44558, due for withdrawal in December.

5th September, 1964.

1964
THE LAST YEAR OF THE S&D 7Fs

Undoubtedly one of the saddest events of the year was the withdrawal from service, on 5th September, of the last surviving S&D 7F 2-8-0 No. 53807. For 50 years these excellent engines had given outstanding service to the Somerset and Dorset but never again would the Mendip Hills echo to the distinctive, striving, exhaust beat of a hard-working S&D 7F, as she toiled up a long stretch of 1 in 50 towards Masbury Summit with a heavy freight.

In April, BR Standard Class 5 No. 73050, which had been one of the three brand new Standard Class 5s allocated to the Somerset and Dorset in the late spring of 1954, was transferred away from the S&D. Then in December, S&D 4F No. 44558 was withdrawn from service, which left just No. 44560 as the final survivor of these versatile 0-6-0s, five of which had been built specially for the Somerset and Dorset in 1922 by Armstrong Whitworth & Co. None remained on the S&D after the end of the year, as, in November, No. 44560 had been transferred from Templecombe to Gloucester Shed.

Ironically, an acute shortage of motive power in the early summer led to a request being made, in May, for the loan of a Standard Class 5 for a short period. However, as had happened in the previous year, the Western Region said they were unable to spare a Class 5 for the S&D, and instead sent over to Bath on loan from Newport (Ebbw Junction) two 9F 2-10-0s, Nos. 92214 and 92226. No. 92214 remained at Bath until late June, working passenger trains over the S&D, but the stay for No. 92226 was shorter, and after only three weeks she was returned to Newport. Whilst at Bath Motive Power Depot, her main use was helping out with the working of northbound freights up the Midland line, with occasional turns on the 6.25p.m. Bath, Green Park, to Avonmouth freight. I personally never saw her used over the S&D during her brief stay at Bath.

Throughout 1964, the deliberate run down of the Somerset and Dorset continued and from 7th September, the line was closed at night, resulting in the withdrawal of all night freights, including the 2.40a.m. "Down Mail", the mails being handed over to road transport for the continuation of their journey south.

Sadly, the once proud Somerset and Dorset was being slowly, but surely, reduced to a state of near impotence.

94. Journey's end. Some of the S&D's ex-GWR 0-6-0s are seen passing through Bitton, on a foggy morning in April, on their last melancholy journey to the breaker's yard.

7th April, 1964.

95. The final run of the last 9F 2-10-0 to be allocated to the Somerset and Dorset. On Saturday, 20th June, No. 92214 was put on the 9.55a.m. down semi-fast from Bath to Bournemouth and then in the afternoon she worked back to Bath with the 3.40p.m.: the "Up Mail". This was the last regular run over the Somerset and Dorset by a 9F 2-10-0. At the beginning of the following week, she was transferred away from Bath Depot. No. 92214 is seen standing in Shillingstone Station. *(See also pictures 131, 132, 139, 143 and 146).*

20th June, 1964.

FAREWELL

96.

The end of the Somerset and Dorset's 7Fs. On Sunday morning, 6th September, the day after making her final run over the Somerset and Dorset, the last of the S&D's 7Fs, No. 53807, stands cold and forlorn on Bath Shed. Standing beside her is Bath's Shedmaster, Mr. Harold Morris. *(See pictures 114 to 118).*

6th September, 1964.

EXCURSIONS AND SCHOOL SPECIALS – THE ONLY TRAINS THAT NOW REQUIRED DOUBLE–HEADING OVER THE MENDIPS

97. On Monday, 20th July, a school special was run from Christchurch to Bath. BR Class 4 4-6-0 No. 75007 and SR Pacific No. 34029 "Lundy" are seen here leaving Bath with the special in the early evening on the return run to Christchurch.

20th July, 1964.

98. The same train being held briefly at Bath Junction, waiting to get the road for the 4 mile single line section down to Midford.

20th July, 1964.

WHIT MONDAY EXCURSION

99. 8F 2-8-0 No. 48660 and BR Class 5 No. 73049 run down past the grounds of Midford Castle, with a Whit Monday excursion from Bath, down to Bournemouth. The photographer on the left is my friend, Norman Lockett, who accompanied me on many of my expeditions.

18th May, 1964.

SCHOOL SPECIAL

100.

BR Class 4 4-6-0 No. 75007 and SR Pacific No. 34079 "141 Squadron", pass Bath Junction, in the evening, with the return working of a school special from Cole to Coventry.

16th July, 1964.

101. No. 80081 stands in Bath, Green Park, Station at the head of the 4.21 p.m. down semi-fast for Bournemouth West.
15th September, 1964.

THE BR STANDARD 2-6-4 TANKS

These versatile engines begin to be used on an increasing variety of turns over the S&D.

102.
No. 80067 pulls away from Midford with the 3.20 p.m. down stopping train.
13th June, 1964.

INTERESTING Ex-GWR VISITORS TO BATH, GREEN PARK

103.

A pigeon special arrives at Bath, Green Park, from the Midlands, hauled by ex-GWR 4-6-0 No. 6871 "Bourton Grange". The train, after setting back off the main line, is seen here drawing forward on the S&D goods approach road for the release of the birds in the south yard.

1st August, 1964.

104. This is thought to have been the only appearance of a Great Western "Castle" at Bath, Green Park. An enthusiasts' special, having run in from the south behind two ex-S&D engines, is taken over by No. 7023 "Penrice Castle", for the continuation of the run north, up to Gloucester. To be strictly accurate, No. 7023 was not an ex-GWR engine, having been completed at Swindon in June 1949, after the Great Western Railway had been nationalized.

7th June, 1964.

BATH, GREEN PARK, MOTIVE POWER DEPOT

105. A line up of locomotives outside the S&D shed. An ex-S&D 4F 0-6-0 No. 44560, two ex-LMS Stanier 8F 2-8-0s, Nos. 48737 and 48431, and BR Standard Class 3 2-6-2T No. 82041.

12th February, 1964.

106. A rare visitor to Bath. Eastern Region Class B1 4-6-0 No. 61143 stands alongside S&D 7F 2-8-0 No. 53807.

12th February, 1964.

'JINTY' PARADE

107. No. 47506 emerges from the old Midland shed. On the left is type 4 "Peak" class diesel No. D44, from Derby shed (16C), which had worked in with a parcels train from the north.
12th February, 1964.

108.

The snow plough engine for the winter of 1963/4: No. 47623.
1st February, 1964.

109.

No. 47276 standing outside the Midland shed.
26th September, 1964.

BATH MOTIVE POWER DEPOT

110. A 'bird's-eye' view of the Midland shed on a quiet Sunday afternoon. In the foreground, standing at the head of a line of withdrawn ex-LMS Stanier type locomotives, is S&D 7F No. 53807, the last surviving member of this class. She had only just been withdrawn herself, having been taken out of service the previous day, Saturday, 5th September. Also in the picture are ex-GWR pannier tank No. 8745 and BR Class 5 No. 73092.
6th September, 1964.

111.

Ex-LMS 4F 0-6-0 No. 44102 stands at the entrance to the south goods yard.
1st February, 1964.

112. Ex-GWR "Grange" class 4-6-0 No. 6871 "Bourton Grange" is being turned after bringing in a pigeon special from the Midlands.
1st August, 1964.

BATH's 60FT. TURNTABLE

113.
After arriving with an up goods and having turned their 8F, No. 48737, Driver Norman Gibbons and Fireman Allen Jeffries pose for me in front of their 8F.
15th September, 1964.

THE FINAL RUN OF THE LAST OF THE S&D 7Fs

On her final day in service, Saturday, 5th September, 1964, No. 53807, the last surviving S&D 7F, worked the 11.00a.m. goods from Bath down to Evercreech Junction and then returned home, 'engine and brake'.

114.

Nearing Moorewood. Although the train was a comparatively heavy one, no banker was taken from Radstock for the 7½ mile climb up the northern slopes of the Mendips.

5th September, 1964.

115.

(Below) Coming up to Masbury Summit, 811 ft. above sea level, after an excellent climb from Radstock.

5th September, 1964.

116. After arriving at Evercreech Junction, and having turned their engine, Driver David Massey and his young fireman, Beverly Reynolds, pose for me in front of No. 53807.

5th September, 1964.

117. Due to lack of traffic, the return working was cancelled and No. 53807 ran back to Bath 'engine and brake'. In this picture, she is passing through Shepton Mallet. The 1.10p.m. down local from Bath was due shortly and seemed to be assured of at least one passenger!

5th September, 1964.

118.

On arriving back at Bath Shed, No. 53807 was turned for the last time. She was then placed on the 'withdrawn' road, and her fire dropped. After 50 years of faithful service, the 7Fs' days on the Somerset and Dorset were over.

5th September, 1964.

ON THE BRANCH – EDINGTON BURTLE

119. On a fine evening in early October, the one van 4.19 p.m. perishables train from Highbridge to Templecombe, hauled by an ex-GWR Collett 0-6-0, passes Edington Burtle's up distant signal. Prior to the take over by the Western Region, this train used to form the late afternoon milk train from Bason Bridge to Templecombe.

3rd October, 1964.

120. Ex-GWR Collett 0-6-0 No. 2218 sets off east from Edington Burtle with the 4.00 p.m. local from Highbridge to Evercreech Junction.

4th August, 1964.

121. Ex-GWR 0-6-0 No. 2218 trundles along beside the South Drain, heading east, away from Catcott Crossing, with the 4.00 p.m. local from Highbridge to Evercreech Junction.
3rd October, 1964.

CATCOTT

122.
Ivatt 2-6-2T No. 41243 runs west from Catcott in charge of the 5.00 p.m. Evercreech Junction to Highbridge local.
3rd October, 1964.

SHAPWICK

123. Ex-GWR 0-6-0 No. 3210 sets off from Shapwick Station and over the level crossing with the 2.20 p.m. Highbridge stopping train to Templecombe. Shapwick's signal box was rather unusual in that it differed in style from other boxes on the line. The lean on the signal, and the train, was due to the unstable nature of the waterlogged sub-terrain in this area. Shapwick was surrounded by peat bogs.

4th August, 1964.

124.

An unpleasant incident. As the 5.00 p.m. stopping train from Evercreech Junction coasts in, drawn by Ivatt 2-6-2T No. 41296, the fireman has the single line token ready to give to the signalman who is standing at the west end of the platform, waiting to exchange tablets as soon as the train has stopped. Although I was in no way obstructing this procedure, which, in any case, was to be carried out with the engine stationary, the driver swore at me in an abusive and exceedingly unpleasant manner as he slowly ran past me. In all my 40 years of taking photographs on the S&D, this was the only occasion on which I was subjected to such abuse. I know the driver's name, but because his attitude was so foreign to the very friendly spirit which always prevailed between the S&D staff and myself, I shall not reveal it, or the date on which this picture was taken.

GLASTONBURY

125. Ex-GWR 0-6-0 No. 2218, engaged in some shunting whilst in charge of an eastbound goods, draws forward past Glastonbury's large and attractive signal box.

8th October, 1964.

PYLLE

126.

Running in behind Ivatt 2-6-2T No. 41296 is the 9.45a.m. local from Highbridge.

8th October, 1964.

127. Ex-GWR 0-6-0 No. 3200, running in from the branch with the 4.00 p.m. local from Highbridge, joins the main line for the final drop down into Evercreech Junction Station.

25th July, 1964.

EVERCREECH JUNCTION

Where the branch ran in to join the main line by the North Box.

128.
The 5.00 p.m. up branch local from Evercreech Junction, hauled by Ivatt 2-6-2T No. 41242, passes the junction bracket signal as she nears the North Box and the start of the run over the branch to Highbridge.

25th July, 1964.

129. BR Class 4 4-6-0 No. 75073, in charge of the 3.40p.m. from Bournemouth, the "Up Mail", draws near to the sharp right hand curve on the main line and the start of the 8½ mile climb, much of it at 1 in 50, up to Masbury Summit. On the left is one of the very distinctive S&D 'calling back' signals. *(See picture 75).*

25th July, 1964.

130. The 4.21 p.m. down semi-fast from Bath, drawn by BR Class 5 4-6-0 No. 73049 carefully rounds the sharp curve by the North Box and starts to coast down the final ¼ mile into Evercreech Junction Station.

25th July, 1964.

A RUN UP THE LINE FROM BOURNEMOUTH WEST TO COLE

BOURNEMOUTH WEST

THE LAST 9F 2-10-0 TO BE ALLOCATED TO BATH DEPOT MAKES HER FINAL RUN OVER THE S&D

On Saturday, 20th June, 9F No. 92214 was put in charge of the 3.40 p.m. from Bournemouth West: the "Up Mail". This was the last run of a 9F* over the S&D and I chased No. 92214 by car from Bournemouth as far as Wellow, securing many shots of her in the course of the journey. *(See pictures 131, 132, 139, 143 and 146).*

Having a 'dice' with a 9F which was being driven by a determined and sporting crew, called for some very fast motoring. Flashing through one village at a speed somewhat in excess of the legal limit, I passed a policeman leaning on his bicycle, having a chat with a villager. Looking hastily in my rear mirror, I just caught a glimpse of the 'bobby' letting his bicycle fall to the ground, and reaching for his notebook! For weeks afterwards I waited for what I thought must be the inevitable call from the police, but it never came!

* There was one more appearance of a 9F on the S&D in 1965 when one hauled an enthusiasts' excursion southwards from Bath, but she was in poor condition and put up a pathetic performance compared with the S&D's own 9F exploits of the past.

131. 9F 2-10-0 No. 92214 backs down into Bournemouth West to couple on to the 3.40 p.m. for Bath: the "Up Mail". Being propelled out of the station and up the bank to the carriage washing plant is the stock of the down "Bournemouth Belle" from Waterloo.

20th June, 1964.

132. 9F No. 92214 makes a vigorous departure from Bournemouth West with the "Up Mail". This was this engine's last run over the Somerset and Dorset before being transferred away from Bath, Green Park, Depot.

20th June, 1964.

PARKSTONE BANK

For the first eight miles of their journey from Bournemouth West up 'to Bath, Somerset and Dorset trains ran over Southern lines. The S&D's own track did not commence until Broadstone.

Parkstone Bank came some two miles after setting off from Bournemouth West. After passing through Branksome, the line began to descend westwards at 1 in 130 and then fell steeply on a ruling gradient of 1 in 60 for over a mile down Parkstone Bank towards Poole. For northbound trains this came as a pleasant, exhilarating downhill frolic, but for southbound Somerset and Dorset trains nearing the end of their run down from Bath, Parkstone Bank presented S&D enginemen with one last major challenge before they finally reached their journey's end at Bournemouth West.

133. The 11.40a.m. up from Bournemouth West, hauled by BR Class 4 2-6-0 No. 76065, in the charge of veteran S&D Driver Donald Beale, drifts down the bank on a lovely morning in early August.
3rd August, 1964.

134. An unusual working for an 8F 2-8-0. On August Bank Holiday Monday, Bath Depot put one of their 8Fs, No. 48470 on the 6.55a.m. down stopping train from Bath to Bournemouth West. The 8F is seen here coming up Parkstone Bank with her lightweight load of three coaches. An added interest concerning No. 48470 is that she was one of a batch of eighty Stanier-designed LMS 8F 2-8-0s that was constructed by the GWR at Swindon Works during World War II. The inset picture on the left shows the maker's plate carried by these GWR built LMS 8Fs.
3rd August, 1964.

135. BR Class 5 No. 73051 coasts down the bank towards Poole with the 4.13 p.m. Evercreech Junction to Bournemouth West stopping train. This was the train run for passengers who had de-trained from the down "Pines Express" at Evercreech Junction for destinations which lay south of the junction where the "Pines" did not stop. Although two years had now passed since the "Pines" ceased to run over the S&D, the Western Region still kept this train in the timetable, following a 'ghost' "Pines" down to Bournemouth and, on most occasions, running virtually empty.

18th April, 1964.

BROADSTONE BANK

Shortly after Poole, the Southern's main line to Weymouth swung away to the west at Holes Bay Junction, the line sweeping round a long curve carried on a low causeway towards Hamworthy Junction. S&D trains kept to the SR line, heading north for Broadstone, and after a mile's running on the level, they came to the foot of Broadstone Bank, which climbed for two miles at 1 in 75 up to Broadstone Junction.

136.

The 5.30 p.m. Bournemouth West to Templecombe, comes smartly up Broadstone Bank, hauled by Ivatt 2-6-2T No. 41243.

18th April, 1964.

BROADSTONE

Broadstone Junction was a busy spot. The Southern line which had climbed up from Poole, joined the one from Hamworthy Junction to Wimborne and Brockenhurst, whilst the S&D's own track, initially single, also commenced at this point swinging away to the north towards Corfe Mullen.

137. BR Class 5 No. 73054, in charge of the "Up Mail", about to swing left on to the S&D's own track. This was single line for the first three miles as far as Corfe Mullen. The mechanical catcher arm has been placed in position on the Class 5 to pick up the tablet from the lineside apparatus.

18th April, 1964.

138.

BR Class 5 No. 73047 runs in with the 4.21 p.m. down semi-fast from Bath to Bournemouth West. The train is coming off the S&D's own single line from Corfe Mullen and has just swung left to join the Southern's line down to Poole.

18th April, 1964.

SHILLINGSTONE

139. The final run over the S&D of the last 9F allocated to Bath Depot. No. 92214 gets away from Shillingstone with the "Up Mail" like 'a shot out of a gun'. I was chasing her by car and, despite some very rapid motoring, she beat me to Sturminster Newton and Stalbridge. However, I just managed to arrive first at Henstridge. The 9F's very sporting crew who, incidentally, were not S&D enginemen but came from Bournemouth Central Depot and were booked to work the train as far as Templecombe, were Driver Arthur Cooper and Fireman Alan Letchford.

20th June, 1964.

140.

The sun did not always shine at Shillingstone! In pouring rain, S&D engines, 7F No. 53807 and 4F No. 44558, pass through Shillingstone on their way, light engine, down to Bournemouth Central. Earlier in the morning they had worked the 8.15a.m. stopping train from Bath down to Templecombe *(see picture 150)*. The next day, Sunday, 7th June, they were scheduled to haul an enthusiasts' special from Bournemouth Central up to Bath, Green Park.

6th June, 1964.

141. BR Class 5 No. 73068 drifts in with the 4.13p.m. down stopping train from Evercreech Junction to Bournemouth West. As usual, the train appeared to be virtually empty. At Shillingstone, no one boarded the train, and no one got off.
18th May, 1964.

142. The 5.30p.m. up stopping train, from Bournemouth West to Templecombe, sets off from Shillingstone, hauled by BR Standard Class 4 2-6-4T No. 80067, a class becoming increasingly popular for use over the Somerset and Dorset.
18th May, 1964.

HENSTRIDGE

143. As No. 92214 departed from Henstridge with the "Up Mail", I waved goodbye to Driver Cooper and Fireman Letchford, for the 'race' was now over. No. 92214 would be handed over to an S&D crew, at Templecombe, for the continuation of the run up to Bath, whilst they were booked to return home to Bournemouth with a southbound train. It is amusing to note that the Southern crew have already placed the single line tablet in the catcher which, strictly speaking, was distinctly against the rules! The tablet should not have been put out before passing Templecombe up distant signal.

20th June, 1964.

APPROACHING TEMPLECOMBE

144.
9F No. 92214, again with the 3.40p.m. up from Bournemouth West, but on a dull day some four weeks earlier, runs north from Henstridge towards Templecombe.
23rd May, 1964.

NEAR SHEPTON MONTAGUE

145. 4F No. 44422, the 4F which has been preserved by the North Staffordshire Railway Society, nears Shepton Montague whilst in charge of the 4.15 p.m. from Templecombe to Bath.

19th May, 1964.

NORTH OF WINCANTON

146. 9F No. 92214, now in the hands of an S&D crew, heads away north from Wincanton with the "Up Mail" on her last run over the Somerset and Dorset. The train's call at Templecombe Upper had made it easy for me to get well ahead of her, and with the arduous climb over the Mendips ahead, everything was now in my favour and I obtained several more pictures of the train on the run up to Bath.

20th June, 1964.

147. Our friend, the "Up Mail" again, this time in the charge of a B R Class 5 No. 73047, emerges from the short cutting near Pitcombe as she heads towards Cole.

19th May, 1964.

NEARING COLE

148. Running through the deep cutting just south of Cole, the driver of Ivatt 2-6-2T No. 41242 has already closed the regulator as he prepares to stop at Cole with the afternoon local from Templecombe to Highbridge.

19th May, 1964.

149. On a lovely sunny afternoon in mid-May, B R Class 5 No. 73068 sets off from Cole with the 4.13 p.m. down stopping train from Evercreech Junction to Bournemouth West.

19th May, 1964.

COLE

The end of our 1964 journey from Bournemouth West up the southern half of the S&D. This would seem to be the appropriate spot at which to conclude our run, for Cole marked the northern extremity of the Dorset Central Railway and it was here, in 1862, that this line linked up with the Somerset Central Railway to form the Somerset and Dorset Railway.

150.

In sharp contrast to the picture above, two S&D engines, 7F No. 53807 and 4F No. 44558 depart in pouring rain with the 8.15 a.m. local from Bath to Templecombe. Later in the day, they set off from Templecombe, light engine, for the run to Bournemouth Central, as on the next day, Sunday, 7th June, they were rostered to haul an enthusiasts' special over the S&D from Bournemouth Central to Bath, Green Park *(see picture 140)*.

6th June, 1964

151. A brief 'cold snap' in early March resulted in much of Somerset lying under an unexpected mantle of snow. On a bright Saturday afternoon, two BR Standard locomotives, Class 3 2-6-2T No. 82004 and Class 4 2-6-0 No. 76057, draw near to Midford with the 12 noon up local from Templecombe.

6th March, 1965.

1965

SADNESS AND DESOLATION

As the New Year came in, the once happy 'family spirit', which had prevailed for so many years amongst the staff on the Somerset and Dorset, was slowly turning to one of bitterness and resentment. This was not because of the fact that their line was now obviously heading for closure, but because of the way in which this was being brought about by the Western Region.

Apart from coal from the Radstock and Norton Hill Collieries, all other freight, where possible, had been diverted away from the S&D, and by June, just one goods train per day worked between Bath and Evercreech Junction.

Everywhere now could be seen dereliction and decay. The signal boxes at Chilcompton, Moorewood, Evercreech New and Cole were closed and, in some cases, quickly knocked down and reduced to a pile of rubble. Stations and other buildings had remained unpainted for years. Sidings were being taken out with increasing rapidity and, by April, most goods stations had been closed. Midford, Wellow and Chilcompton had been reduced to unmanned halts, which particularly angered the residents of Wellow who had always given good patronage to their station.

Towards the end of July, the Southern Region announced that Bournemouth West Station would be closed from Monday, 2nd August until Saturday, 4th September whilst engineering works, in connection with the Bournemouth electrification scheme, was carried out. During this period, S&D trains commenced and terminated their journeys at Bournemouth Central, with just a few beginning and ending their runs at Branksome. In the event, Bournemouth West Station never re-opened, the Minister of Transport consenting to its closure on 4th October.

Prior to this, in June, had come the long expected proposals from the Western Region that all passenger services over the Somerset and Dorset system should be withdrawn in September but before any action could be taken, compulsory public meetings had to be held to hear objections to these proposals and, as expected, they were legion. Thereafter, the Transport Users' Consultative Committee held meetings to consider the many objections which had been lodged. Weeks passed with no pronouncement forthcoming. At last came the decision of the Minister of Transport. The Somerset and Dorset would close on 3rd January, 1966. So the battle had finally been lost. Everywhere, sadness and desolation stared one in the face.

152.

In September, 'Jinty' No. 47276 became a temporary 'film star' when she was selected to take part in a railway scene in the film, "The Wrong Box". Her role entailed her being painted green (on the right hand side only) and having her number altered by the simple expediency of painting out the first and last figures. No. 47276, as '727', is seen here, standing in the old Midland shed showing off her temporary green livery. Her companion on the left is an ex-GWR pannier tank.

11th September, 1965.

153. An unexpected Pacific meeting at Bath, Green Park. Southern "West Country" Pacific No. 34046 "Braunton", sets off from Bath with the 4.21 p.m. down semi-fast for Bournemouth, and passes BR "Britannia" Pacific No. 70034 "Thomas Hardy". It was unusual, in 1965, for a Southern Pacific, once almost an everyday sight on the S&D, to appear at Bath. Whereas Bournemouth Central Depot did provide the power for the 4.21 p.m. down, being the return run home for an up working in the morning, a Class 4 was normally considered adequate power for the weight of trains now being run over the S&D. The "West Country" had been pressed into service at short notice due to the non-availability of a Class 4 locomotive. By 1965, the appearance of a "Britannia" at Bath, Green Park, was also most unusual. She had arrived with a down parcels train and, having been turned, was about to return north again; light engine.

1st May, 1965.

BATH DEPARTURES

154.

Smoky departure! As BR Class 4 4-6-0 No. 75072 leaves with the 4.37p.m. down local, she is 'paced' by 2-6-4T No. 80146 moving forward from the turntable. On the left is the rare visitor from the north, "Britannia" Pacific No. 70034 "Thomas Hardy". The "Britannia" Pacifics were barred from working south of Bath over the S&D due to their axle loading.

1st May, 1965.

THE 6.05 p.m. (SX) BATH TO BINEGAR LOCAL

By 1965, this had been reduced to just one coach and was usually worked by a B R Standard Class 3 2-6-2 tank.

155. Drifting down past the grounds of Midford Castle with No. 82041 in charge.
10th May, 1965.

156.

No. 82004 sets off briskly from Wellow with her one coach.
25th May, 1965.

157.

Emerging from Chilcompton Tunnel, hauled by No. 82004.
13th May, 1965.

THE BR STANDARD CLASS 4 2-6-4 TANKS

These versatile locomotives were now being used for many services over the S&D.

158. The 4.15p.m. up from Templecombe, hauled by No. 80059, climbs towards Winsor Hill Tunnel on a lovely spring afternoon in early April.

10th April, 1965.

159.

No. 80043, having just called at Midsomer Norton, coasts down past Norton Hill Colliery with the 9.05a.m. up stopping train from Templecombe.

7th June, 1965.

160. No. 76006 climbs up out of Chilcompton Tunnel with the 1.10 p.m. down local from Bath, Green Park.
28th December, 1965.

THE B R STANDARD CLASS 4 2-6-0s

Although in 1965 several services over the S&D were regularly rostered for a B R Class 4 2-6-0, this power was always provided by Bournemouth Central or, occasionally, Eastleigh Motive Power Depot. No engines of this class were ever allocated to an S&D shed.

161.

(Below) The 1.10 p.m. up from Bournemouth, hauled by No. 76057, is framed by trees as she passes through the lovely countryside near Wellow on her way to Bath. Since early August, this train had to commence its journey from Branksome whilst the normal departure point, Bournemouth West Station, was 'temporarily' closed in connection with the Bournemouth electrification scheme. In the event, this station was never re-opened.
18th September, 1965.

TWO OF THE S&D's BR STANDARD CLASS 5s

162. On a lovely calm evening in late August, BR Class 5 No. 73068 passes by, running north over Cole Viaduct with the 3.40p.m., the "Up Mail", from Bournemouth. However, it was cool down by the river that ran beneath the viaduct – and the best of the summer was over.

31st August, 1965.

163.

BR Class 5 No. 73051 leaves Cole in charge of the 9.55a.m. down from Bath. By now, very little goods traffic was left on the S&D and station goods yards were being closed and were having their sidings lifted at an ever increasing rate. However, because of a local coal merchant's contract, one siding at Cole still survived in the summer of 1965. No. 73051 was one of the original BR Standard Class 5s allocated, brand-new, to Bath Depot in May 1954. Although only just over eleven years old, and still in good condition, she was withdrawn from service and broken up just one month after this picture was taken.

17th July, 1965.

BR STANDARD CLASS 4 4-6-0 No. 75072

164. No. 75072, with the 4.37 p.m. Bath to Templecombe local, drifts down over Tucking Mill Viaduct, an idyllic and totally peaceful spot set amidst the trees in Horsecombe Vale.
31st March, 1965.

In June 1956, Bath Motive Power Depot had been allocated three Standard Class 4 4-6-0s, Nos. 75071, 75072 and 75073 and all three, during their periodic visits to Eastleigh for overhaul, were converted to the double blast pipe and chimney arrangement. However, by 1965, only No. 75072 still remained on the S&D and she was no longer shedded at Bath, but had been transferred to Templecombe. These four pictures show her on a variety of turns.

165.

The 12 noon from Templecombe, in the charge of No. 75072, emerges from Devonshire Tunnel and coasts down the 1 in 50 bank into Bath.
10th April, 1965.

166. A 'skyline' view of No. 75072 as, blowing off after the 1 in 60 descent towards Midford, she prepares to stop at Midford Station with the 4.15 p.m. up local from Templecombe.

20th May, 1965.

167. After climbing for 7½ miles, much of it at 1 in 50, No. 75072 passes over Masbury Summit whilst in charge of the 4.37 p.m. stopping train from Bath to Templecombe.

12th June, 1965.

THE DECIMATION OF THE S&D's GOODS TRAFFIC

By 1965 the Western Region had succeeded in diverting away, from the Somerset and Dorset, nearly all goods traffic. From June 1965, the position had been reached where just one daily down goods train per day sufficed to carry what little traffic remained.

168. Ex-LMS Stanier 8F 2-8-0 No. 48444 emerges from Chilcompton Tunnel with the once daily down goods from Bath. No. 48444 was of particular interest in that she was one of a wartime batch of Stanier-designed LMS 8Fs built at Swindon Works *(see inset to picture 134).*
31st August, 1965.

169. The same train coming up to Masbury Summit. This day's working was unusual as the train was booked to run down the line as far south as Wincanton.
31st August, 1965.

170.

The sadness and desolation of the S&D. As 8F No. 48309 sets off from Chilcompton with the 1.10 p.m. down local, she passes a pile of rubble in the foreground. This was all that remained of Chilcompton's once attractive small signal box which had been closed in April and recently demolished. By the autumn of 1965, demolition of S&D signal boxes and other buildings was being ruthlessly pursued in anticipation of the impending closure of the Somerset and Dorset line.

9th October, 1965.

AN 8F 2-8-0 ON PASSENGER WORK

By the autumn of 1965, the situation concerning motive power on the S&D had been reached where the use of an 8F 2-8-0 on a passenger train no longer caused any comment.

171. The same train at Shepton Mallet. No. 48309 was an interesting Stanier 8F in that she was one of only two engines, the other being No. 48728, of this class to have been equipped with steam-heating apparatus. This was fitted when these two 8Fs had been prepared for hauling the "Royal Train" on a journey, through Wales, some years earlier.

9th October, 1965.

172.

Ivatt 2-6-2T No. 41216 approaches Elbow Corner Crossing with a Highbridge-bound local. On the left is Evercreech Junction North's down distant signal, whilst the train has just passed Elbow Corner's up home signal. Usually on the S&D, manned crossings situated within block sections, had their own signals, both distant and home, worked from a ground frame at the crossing. Elbow Corner Crossing was an exception in having only home signals, and no distants.

12th June, 1965.

THE HIGHBRIDGE–TEMPLECOMBE SERVICE – scenes on the Branch

173. The one van afternoon 'perishables' from Highbridge, hauled by Ivatt 2-6-2T No. 41242, has just passed Edington Burtle's up distant signal and is drawing near to Catcott Crossing.

3rd April, 1965.

IN PYLLE WOODS

174.
Ex-GWR pannier tank No. 4631 climbs up through Pylle Woods with the 2.20p.m. from Highbridge to Templecombe.
12th June, 1965.

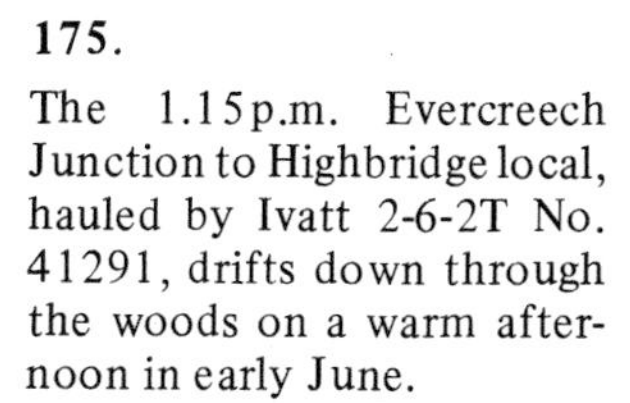
175.
The 1.15p.m. Evercreech Junction to Highbridge local, hauled by Ivatt 2-6-2T No. 41291, drifts down through the woods on a warm afternoon in early June.
7th June, 1965.

THE HIGHBRIDGE–TEMPLECOMBE SERVICE

176.

The 2.20p.m. from Highbridge comes up the bank, much of it at 1 in 88, through Pylle Woods, hauled by ex-GWR Collett 0-6-0 No. 3205. This engine has been preserved and is now running, in immaculate condition, on the Severn Valley Railway.

3rd April, 1965.

177.

Ivatt 2-6-2T No. 41296 in charge of the afternoon local from Templecombe to Highbridge, passes under Wyke Champflower Bridge, which carried, over the line, the lane leading to Castle Cary. This bridge, No. 115 in the official S&D bridge list, is of interest because, unlike other stone bridges over the S&D, it was built to span double track. The whole of the Somerset and Dorset was originally built as a single line and when, in later years, sections of it came to be doubled, the usual procedure at bridges, which, of course, had been constructed to cross over just one line, was to build a second span alongside the original one.

15th May, 1965.

EVERCREECH JUNCTION

178. BR Standard Class 4 2-6-4T No. 80134 sets off for Bath with the 11.40a.m. from Bournemouth, whilst standing in the middle road is Ivatt 2-6-2T No. 41291 with the stock to form the 1.15p.m. over the branch to Highbridge. As soon as the Bath train had departed, the Ivatt drew her stock forward on to the main line and then set back into the up platform. I often wondered why, over the years, a line was never put in against the outer face of the up platform for use by the branch line trains.

7th June, 1965.

179.

Ex-GWR pannier tank No. 4631 sets off from the junction with the 2.20p.m. local from Highbridge to Templecombe.

12th June, 1965.

WHIT MONDAY EXCURSIONS DOWN TO BOURNEMOUTH FROM BATH AND BRISTOL

These were destined to be the last excursions to terminate at Bournemouth West for, although it was not known at the time, Bournemouth West was to be closed on 2nd August. Both trains were absolutely full, for these excursions remained as popular as ever right up to the end, which was not really so surprising as the return fare from Bath was only fifteen shillings (75p in modern money). How far could one travel for this amount today?

180. The Bath excursion, hauled by BR Class 5 No. 73051, climbs towards Moorewood. This train left Bath at 9.35a.m. and, after calling at most stations down the line as far south as Evercreech Junction, arrived at Bournemouth West at 12.12p.m. The return train set off from Bournemouth West at 7.10p.m.

7th June, 1965.

181.

Two BR Standard type 4-6-0s, Class 4 No. 75009 and Class 5 No. 73054, emerge from Combe Down Tunnel into the sunshine of Horsecombe Vale with the excursion from Bristol.

7th June, 1965.

182. The excursion from Bath, which had eight on and was headed by BR Class 5 No. 73001, descends towards Midford.

30th August, 1965.

THE TWO FINAL BANK HOLIDAY EXCURSIONS TO RUN OVER THE S&D FROM BATH AND BRISTOL DOWN TO BOURNEMOUTH

These two excursions, both filled to capacity, ran on the August Bank Holiday which the Government had changed from the long traditional first Monday in August to the last Monday in the month. As Bournemouth West had been closed by this date, both trains terminated at Bournemouth Central.

183. The excursion from Bristol climbs the 1 in 50 towards Midsomer Norton. This train, hauled by BR Class 5 No. 73068, was made up to ten bogies and so needed assistance over the Mendips from Bath down to Evercreech Junction. This produced an unusual locomotive combination as the pilot provided by Bath Shed was a BR Standard Class 4 2-6-4T No. 80059.

30th August, 1965.

ENTHUSIASTS' SPECIALS

As the end of the Somerset and Dorset drew ever closer, more and more enthusiasts' specials were run over the line.

184. Passing Henstridge. As far as Templecombe, the train was hauled by BR Standard Class 5 No. 73022.

28th March, 1965.

185. Coming up through the trees at Wyke Champflower. Engines had been changed at Templecombe, and ex-S&D 4F No. 44560, specially loaned by Gloucester Shed to the S&D for the occasion, was in charge of the excursion from Templecombe to Highbridge and back.

28th March, 1965.

"The Southern Wanderer" organized by the Southern Counties Touring Society, started from London, Victoria. The train ran down to Bournemouth and then up the S&D to Evercreech Junction and over the branch to Highbridge. From Highbridge, the excursion then ran back down the S&D to Templecombe from where it returned to London over the Southern main line.

186.

Nearing Catcott on the outward run over the branch to Highbridge.

28th March, 1965.

187.

The return run. With the late afternoon shadows lengthening, the excursion passes Horsington as it draws near to Templecombe.

28th March, 1965.

188. Heading east from Templecombe. For the final fast run back to London over the Southern main line, the engine in charge was SR Pacific No. 35023 "Holland-Afrika Line". Although the "Merchant Navy" Pacifics were officially barred from working over the S&D, due to their axle loading, special dispensation had been given for No. 35023 to work, light engine, from Bournemouth up to Templecombe earlier in the day, so as to be available for hauling the special back to London in the evening.

28th March, 1965.

ENTHUSIASTS' SPECIAL – " THE WESSEX DOWNSMAN"

This excursion was organized by the Locomotive Club of Great Britain, and the route was arranged to include a run south over the Somerset and Dorset.

189. Ex-LMS 8F 2-8-0 No. 48309, which had been beautifully turned out, waits to take over the special for the run south over the S&D. No. 48309 had the unusual feature of being fitted with steam heating facilities, one of only two Stanier 8F 2-8-0s so equipped.

2nd May, 1965.

190.
Ex-LMS 4F 0-6-0 No. 44264, running into Bath from the north with the special, passes by the 8F which would be taking the train south.

2nd May, 1965.

191. 8F 2-8-0 No. 48309 sets off from Bath, Green Park, with the special for the run south over the Somerset and Dorset.

2nd May, 1965.

192.
Coming up through Midsomer Norton on the 7½ mile climb from Radstock up to Masbury Summit, 811ft. above sea level.

2nd May, 1965.

193. Running far behind schedule, 9F 2-10-0 No. 92238 looms slowly out of the low cloud enveloping Masbury Summit and coasts downhill, with the special, towards Masbury Halt.

12th June, 1965.

THE WARWICKSHIRE RAILWAY SOCIETY SPECIAL

This society had very bad luck for their special organized for 12th June. A part of the route was over the S&D and although the date was near midsummer, the weather was miserable with Masbury Summit enveloped in thick cloud. Added to this, arrangements had been made to 'import' a 9F specially to haul their train over the S&D and its performance was absolutely abysmal. The climb up the northern slopes of the Mendips was painfully slow, with the speed dropping, at times, to little above walking pace.

194.

Much later in the day, after the cloud had lifted, the 9F was observed passing slowly over Masbury Summit, returning home, light engine.

12th June, 1965.

**AS THE AUTUMN MISTS START TO FORM,
THE END DRAWS NEAR FOR THE SOMERSET AND DORSET**

195. The 1.10p.m. up from Branksome, hauled by a BR Standard Class 4 2-6-0, runs through the thickening mist towards Wellow.
23rd October, 1965.

196.

BR Standard Class 4 2-6-4T No. 80039 heads south from Wellow into the growing gloom with the 3.20p.m. down stopping train from Bath.
23rd October, 1965.

MY LAST FOOTPLATE RUN OVER THE S&D (VERY NEARLY IN MORE WAYS THAN ONE!)

With the end of the S&D drawing near, I asked the Divisional Public Relations Officer, Bristol, if I might be allowed the privilege of a final footplate journey from Bath down to Bournemouth. To my delight my request was granted. I was issued with a footplate permit for the 9.55a.m. down from Bath to Branksome on 1st December 1965. By this date, Bournemouth West had already been closed.

At 9.30a.m. on Wednesday, 1st December, a cold and misty morning, I arrived on Bath Shed to be greeted by my friend, Shedmaster Harold Morris who introduced me to Locomotive Inspector Francomb who was to accompany me on the run.

Our locomotive was BR Standard Class 5 No. 73001, one of the first of the class to be built, having entered service in May 1951, and a fairly recent transfer to Bath Depot. To add to my pleasure, I found that the driver, as far as Templecombe, was an old friend of mine, Driver Ray Stokes, with, as his mate, a very keen young fireman, Robin Gould.

197. BR Standard Class 5 No. 73001 stands in disgrace at Midsomer Norton after the 'blow back'.

1st December, 1965.

All went well as far as Midsomer Norton, with no hint given of what was about to occur. The approach to this station was on a rising grade of 1 in 50, which eased off briefly to 1 in 300 through the platforms, with the result that drivers tended to keep steam on until just short of the station.

As we neared the start of the platform, Ray Stokes turned on the blower, closed the regulator and had just applied the brake when, with horrifying suddenness, an inferno erupted from the open firebox doors and the cab was engulfed in flames. We had suffered a monumental 'blow back'. By the grace of God, none of the four of us was standing in the middle of the cab. Inspector Francomb and Fireman Gould were looking out of the right hand side of the cab, whilst I was standing behind Ray, peering through the left hand spectacle. Ray having just applied the brake, the train was already slowing down when Inspector Francomb and Robin Gould hurriedly 'abandoned ship' on the right hand side, whilst Ray and I departed from the left hand side of the cab.

None of us suffered more than a singeing apart from Robin Gould who had minor burns to his hands. It had been a very lucky escape and had the trouble occurred earlier, in Combe Down Tunnel, you would not be reading this now!

With all four of us safely off the engine, which had shuddered to a stop, it quickly became clear that this was no ordinary 'blow back' for, although the blower was full on, the flames showed no signs of dying down. As a later examination revealed, what in fact had occurred was that the steam pipe to the blower had fractured in the smokebox, so with the blower full on, it was having just the opposite effect to that desired!

198. No. 73001 is left in the entrance to Midsomer Norton's small goods yard, whilst the 'commandeered' Stanier 8F No. 48760 sets back on to our train.

1st December, 1965.

199. The 8F takes water at Evercreech Junction. Although No. 48760 steamed well, she was a real 'bone shaker', riding very roughly, but the old girl got us safely to Templecombe.

1st December, 1965.

Soon someone found a shunter's pole and, with this, the crew managed to close the firebox doors. Earlier on, the engine had been uncoupled from the train, and after about twenty minutes things had cooled down sufficiently for Ray Stokes pluckily to climb back aboard, using old sacking to mask him from the tremendous heat still in the cab. Having turned off the blower, he then drove the engine forward and dropped it back into the entrance to Midsomer Norton's small goods yard.

In the meantime, Inspector Francomb had found a Stanier 8F 2-8-0 shunting Norton Hill Colliery Yard which was just to the north of the station and he 'commandeered' this engine for our train. So on to this old girl the four of us clambered and off we set for Templecombe, where we duly arrived one hour late and with our unfortunate passengers blue with cold, as the 8F had no steam heating facilities. Of the rest of the journey, down to Branksome, I remember little except that it was with a new crew on a Standard Class 4; but I shall never forget the experience at Midsomer Norton.

200.

Although they had been through a pretty dramatic experience, both Driver Ray Stokes and Fireman Robin Gould looked out smiling from the 8F's cab as I took this picture of them after our arrival at Templecombe.

1st December, 1965.

201. On the last day of normal service on the branch, Saturday, 1st January 1966, Ivatt 2-6-2T No. 41290 draws near to Glastonbury with the 1.15p.m. from Evercreech Junction. From the following Monday, 3rd January, the Western Region's 'emergency service' for the S&D was to commence and the branch would then have just four trains a day: two up and two down.

1st January, 1966.

1966

THE END OF THE LINE

The Western Region had already announced that the closure of the Somerset and Dorset would be on 3rd January, when, at the 'eleventh hour' one of the road operators suddenly withdrew his application for a licence to run one of the bus services which was to replace the train service.

Arrangements for an alternative bus service could not be completed in time, so a dying Somerset and Dorset, still worked by steam, had to drag itself on for a few more tormented weeks, much to the embarrassment of the Western Region which had previously announced that 3rd January was 'D' day, when steam would have been eliminated completely from their region and from when all services would be diesel-operated.

For the final few weeks, only a minimal 'emergency service'* was run over the line, interspersed with a number of 'Farewell Specials' chartered by various railway societies. Dereliction and decay had set in everywhere and it was almost with a feeling of relief when the Somerset and Dorset finally died on the evening of Sunday, 6th March 1966.

202. As from 3rd January, the Western Region's 'emergency service' for the S&D had come into force, and Bath, Green Park, was reduced to a service of only four trains down and four trains up per day. One of the up trains, the 2.00p.m. from Templecombe, is seen climbing towards Winsor Hill Tunnel hauled by an unidentified BR Standard Class 4 2-6-0.

26th February, 1966.

* The 'emergency service' timetable is reproduced in the end papers at the back of this book.

203. The LCGB special hauled by SR "Merchant Navy" Pacific No. 35011 "General Steam Navigation", passes Henstridge in the rain. Officially, the "Merchant Navy" Pacifics were barred from running over the S&D because of their axle loading, but with the end of the Somerset and Dorset now so near, such things no longer seemed to matter.

1st January, 1966.

LCGB SPECIAL

Before it was known that the Western Region's closure of the S&D on 3rd January would have to be postponed, the Locomotive Club of Great Britain had arranged a special to be a 'last run' over the line on the Saturday, 1st January, 1966. Notwithstanding the deferment of closure, the running of this train went ahead as planned.

204. Engines were changed at Templecombe, the "Merchant Navy" coming off and being replaced by two Ivatt 2-6-2Ts Nos. 41307 and 41283. The special then set off for the run up to Evercreech Junction and over the branch to Highbridge. With the rain just starting to ease off, the two Ivatts, with their train, are seen here passing over Cole Viaduct.

1st January, 1966.

205. The RCTS special climbs towards Winsor Hill Tunnel. For the run from Bournemouth Central up to Bath, Green Park, the train was hauled by SR 'U' class 2-6-0 No. 31639 and "West Country" Pacific No. 34015 "Exmouth". This photograph was kindly taken for me by Mrs Angela O'Shea, as I was busy filming the train from an adjoining field.

2nd January, 1966.

RCTS SPECIAL

Prior to the Western Region's enforced postponement of the closure of the S&D on 3rd January, 1966, the Railway Correspondence and Travel Society, like the LCGB, had also made arrangements for a last special over the S&D. Their special was to run on the Sunday, 2nd January, and the RCTS also decided to go ahead with the running of their train even though the S&D had been temporarily reprieved for a few weeks. The route followed by the RCTS special differed from that of the LCGB train of the previous day. The RCTS special ran straight up the S&D from Bournemouth to Bath, and then over the Midland line via Mangotsfield to Bristol. From Bristol it travelled down the Western Region main line as far as Highbridge where it rejoined the S&D. The special then ran over the branch to Evercreech Junction and on down to Templecombe from where it returned to London, Victoria, via the Southern main line.

206. Two Ivatt 2-6-2Ts Nos. 41283 and 41307 pass Catcott, light engine, on their way from Templecombe over to Highbridge. On the arrival of the special at Highbridge, they were to take over the train for the run over the branch to Evercreech Junction and on down to Templecombe.

2nd January, 1966.

207. For the run from Bath, Green Park, over the Midland line via Mangotsfield to Bristol, and then down the Western Region main line to Highbridge, the special was hauled by ex-LMS 8F 2-8-0 No. 48309. This was Bath's 8F fitted with steam heating, a facility which, no doubt, pleased the passengers on this cold January day and also probably surprised quite a few, for it was not generally known that there were any Stanier 8F 2-8-0s equipped with steam heating apparatus. No. 48309 is seen here, in charge of the special, running into Highbridge on the Western Region main line. She is just passing over the crossing with the S&D line which ran to Highbridge Wharf and Burnham-on-Sea.

2nd January, 1966.

208.

My last picture of the RCTS special, taken late in the afternoon and, in fact, after moonrise! The train, now headed by the two Ivatt 2-6-2 tanks, is drawing near to Catcott on the run from Highbridge down to Templecombe.

2nd January, 1966.

209. The LCGB special, hauled by two Ivatt 2-6-2Ts Nos. 41307 and 41269, draws near to Glastonbury on the run over the branch from Evercreech Junction to Highbridge and back.

5th March, 1966.

THE LCGB SPECIAL

With the end of the Somerset and Dorset now irrevocably fixed for 7th March, the Locomotive Club of Great Britain organized a 'Farewell' special to run over the line on the last Saturday, 5th March. The special ran down the Southern main line to Templecombe where it as taken over by two absolutely immaculate Bulleid Pacifics; "West Country" No. 34006 "Bude" and "Battle of Britain" No. 34057 "Biggin Hill", for the run up the S&D to Evercreech Junction. At the junction, the Pacifics came off and two Ivatt 2-6-2 tanks then took the special down the branch to Highbridge and back. On the return to the junction, the Pacifics took charge again for the run up to Bath and then in the late afternoon, set off from Bath on the final run south over the Somerset and Dorset.

210. "Bude" and "Biggin Hill" coasting down the northern slopes of the Mendips with the special and drawing near to Moorewood.

5th March, 1966.

211.

Nearing the end of the up run. The special emerges from Devonshire Tunnel and sweeps down the 1 in 50 bank into Bath.

5th March, 1966.

212. My last picture of the special, taken in the late afternoon, as the two beautifully turned out Pacifics, "Bude" and "Biggin Hill", cross over Midford Viaduct with the train on their final run south over the Somerset and Dorset.

5th March, 1966.

THE LAST SATURDAY, 5th MARCH, 1966

213. 2-6-2T No. 41307 and 2-6-4T No. 80138 approach Midford with the 2.00p.m. from Templecombe. With the closure of the line only a day away, as many engines as possible were being worked north so as to be on Bath Depot when the end came.
5th March, 1966.

214. The 4.25p.m. from Bath, Green Park, absolutely packed out with people having their last ride over the Somerset and Dorset, sets off south from Wellow hauled by 2-6-4T No. 80043.
5th March, 1966.

215. My last Somerset and Dorset picture, taken shortly before sunset on Saturday, 5th March. Ex-LMS 8F 2-8-0 No. 48706 draws near to Wellow with the Great Western Society special on the return run from Bournemouth to Bath, Green Park.

5th March, 1966.

NOTE: The last day for the Somerset and Dorset was Sunday, 6th March, but I took no pictures for I was 'otherwise engaged', taking my annual Royal Observer Corps examinations.

Here where steam ruled so well – all is gone,
Tracks lifted; stations demolished – familiar locations
Now unfamiliar – for only the memories remain.
Unique and busy once was this line,
Now made redundant by the march of time.
Never again will the Mendips echo
To the sound of hard pressed "steam".
Now the hills set in mysterious fold,
Watch silently as nature takes her toll –
And the larks' song is the only whistle heard.

From Raymond Lloyd's poem
on the Somerset & Dorset Railway

BRITISH RAILWAYS

WESTERN AND SOUTHERN REGIONS

SOMERSET AND DORSET LINE

REVISION OF PASSENGER TRAIN SERVICES FROM

3rd JANUARY 1966

UNTIL FURTHER NOTICE

Owing to one of the road operators withdrawing his application for a licence to provide some of the alternative road services forming part of the consent conditions laid down by the Minister of Transport and the consequent postponement of the Licensing Court, it has become necessary to defer the date of closure of this line.

A new closing date has yet to be announced, but as from 3rd January, 1966, all existing passenger services between the following places will be suspended. An interim emergency service will be introduced, full details of which are contained in this pamphlet.

The sections of line concerned are:

Bath Green Park to Bournemouth

Highbridge to Evercreech Junction

December 1965 *Paddington and Waterloo*

Printed by J. W. Arrowsmith Ltd., Bristol

REVISED SERVICE - WEEKDAYS ONLY
COMMENCING MONDAY, 3rd JANUARY, 1966

BATH GREEN PARK TO BOURNEMOUTH

Station													SX	SO
BATH GREEN PARK	dep.			06 45		08 15				16 25		18 10		
Midford Halt				06 57		08 27				16 37		18 22		
Wellow Halt				07 03		08 34				16 44		18 29		
Shoscombe & Single Hill Halt				07 07		08 38				16 48		18 33		
Radstock North				07 13		08 44				16 54		18 39		
Midsomer Norton South				07 20		08 51				17 01		18 47		
Chilcompton				07 28		08 59				17 09		18 55		
Binegar				07 36		09 07				17 17		19 03		
Masbury Halt				07 40		09 11				17 21		19 07		
Shepton Mallet Charlton Road				07 50		09 18				17 29		19 15		
Evercreech New				07 56		09 25				17 35		19 21		
Evercreech Junction	arr.			08 00		09 29				17 38		19 24		
Highbridge for Burnham-on-Sea	dep.		06 55						16 00					
Bason Bridge			06 59						16 05					
Edington Burtle			07 05						16 12					
Shapwick Halt			07 10						16 18					
Ashcott			07 17						16 21					
Glastonbury & Street			07 22						16 30					
West Pennard			07 31						16 42					
Pylle Halt			07 40						16 52					
Evercreech Junction	arr.		07 45						17 00					
Evercreech Junction	dep.		07 46	08 04		09 32		16 13		17 43		19 28		
Cole			—	08 13		09 38		16 20		17 48		19 34		
Wincanton			—	08 22		09 47		16 29		17 57		19 43		
TEMPLECOMBE	arr.		08 05	08 29		09 53		16 36		18 05		19 50		
	dep.	07 35			09 05		12 30	16 42					21 03	21 03
Henstridge		07 44			09 14		12 39	16 51					21 11	21 11
Stalbridge		07 51			09 19		12 47	16 55					21 16	21 16
Sturminster Newton		07 59			09 27		12 54	17 06					21 23	21 23
Shillingstone		08 06			09 37		13 00	17 12					21 29	21 29
Blandford Forum		08 17			09 47		13 10	17 22					21 39	21 39
Bailey Gate		08 28			09 59		13 21	17 33			18 32		—	21 50
Broadstone		08 40			10 20		13 32	17 50			18 44		21 58	22 04
Creekmoor Halt		08 44			10 26		13 36	17 54			—		22 02	22 08
Poole		08 49			10 31		13 42	18 02			18 57		22 13	22 13
Parkstone		08 56			10 38		13 47	—			—		—	—
Branksome		09 01			10 42		13 51	18 10			19 06		—	—
BOURNEMOUTH CENTRAL		09 06			—		13 57	18 15			19 11		22 25	22 25

REVISED SERVICE - WEEKDAYS ONLY
COMMENCING MONDAY, 3rd JANUARY, 1966

BOURNEMOUTH TO BATH GREEN PARK

Station										SX		SO			
BOURNEMOUTH CENTRAL	dep.			06b53		09 37		—		15 37		15 43		17 37	18 46
Branksome				07b00		09 44		13 25		15 44		15 50		17 43	18 53
Parkstone				07f05		09 48		13 29		15 48		15 53		17 47	18 57
Poole				07b10		09 53		13 34		15 54		16 00		17 55	19 05
Creekmoor Halt				07b15		09 58		13 39		16 00		16 05		18 01	19 10
Broadstone				07 32		10 02		13 44		16 05		16 09		18 05	19 14
Bailey Gate				07 42		10 12		13 54		16 15		16 19		18 15	19 24
Blandford Forum				07 52		10 25		14 05		16 26		16a30		18 27	19 34
Shillingstone				08 10		10 36		14 15		16 42				18 37	19 44
Sturminster Newton				08 16		10 42		14 21		16a49				18 43	19 50
Stalbridge				08 23		10 49		14 28						18 50	19 57
Henstridge				08 28		10 54		14 33						18 55	20 02
TEMPLECOMBE	arr.			08 37		11 03		14 42						19 04	20 11
	dep.	07 00	08 20				14 00		15 30		16 18				20 20
Wincanton		07 07	08 28				14 06		15 38		16 26				20 27
Cole		07 16	08 39				14 17		15 47		16 34				20 37
Evercreech Junction	arr.	07 23	08 44				14 23		15 53		16 39				20 43
Evercreech Junction	dep.				08 45								17 15		
Pylle Halt					V								17 19		
West Pennard					08 55								17 27		
Glastonbury & Street					09 06								17 38		
Ashcott					09 12								17 46		
Shapwick Halt					09 17								17 51		
Edington Burtle					09 22								17 57		
Bason Bridge					09 28								18 05		
Highbridge for Burnham-on-Sea	arr.				09 33								18 10		
Evercreech Junction	dep.	07 25					14 25				16 40				20 45
Evercreech New		07 31					14 31				16 46				20 51
Shepton Mallet Charlton Road		07 52					14 44				16 59				21 00
Masbury Halt		—					—				17 09				—
Binegar		08 08					14 58				17 15				V
Chilcompton		08 14					15 04				17 21				—
Midsomer Norton South		08 19					15 09				17 26				21 22
Radstock North		08 24					15 14				17 31				21 27
Shoscombe & Single Hill Halt		08 30					15 20				17 37				21 33
Wellow Halt		08 34					15 24				17 41				V
Midford Halt		08 40					15 30				17 47				V
BATH GREEN PARK		08 50					15 40				17 57				21 50

b On Saturdays Bournemouth Central dep. 07 05, Branksome 07 12, Poole 07 19, Creekmoor Halt 07 24. f — **NOT** Saturdays

V — Calls to set down passengers on notice being given to the guard

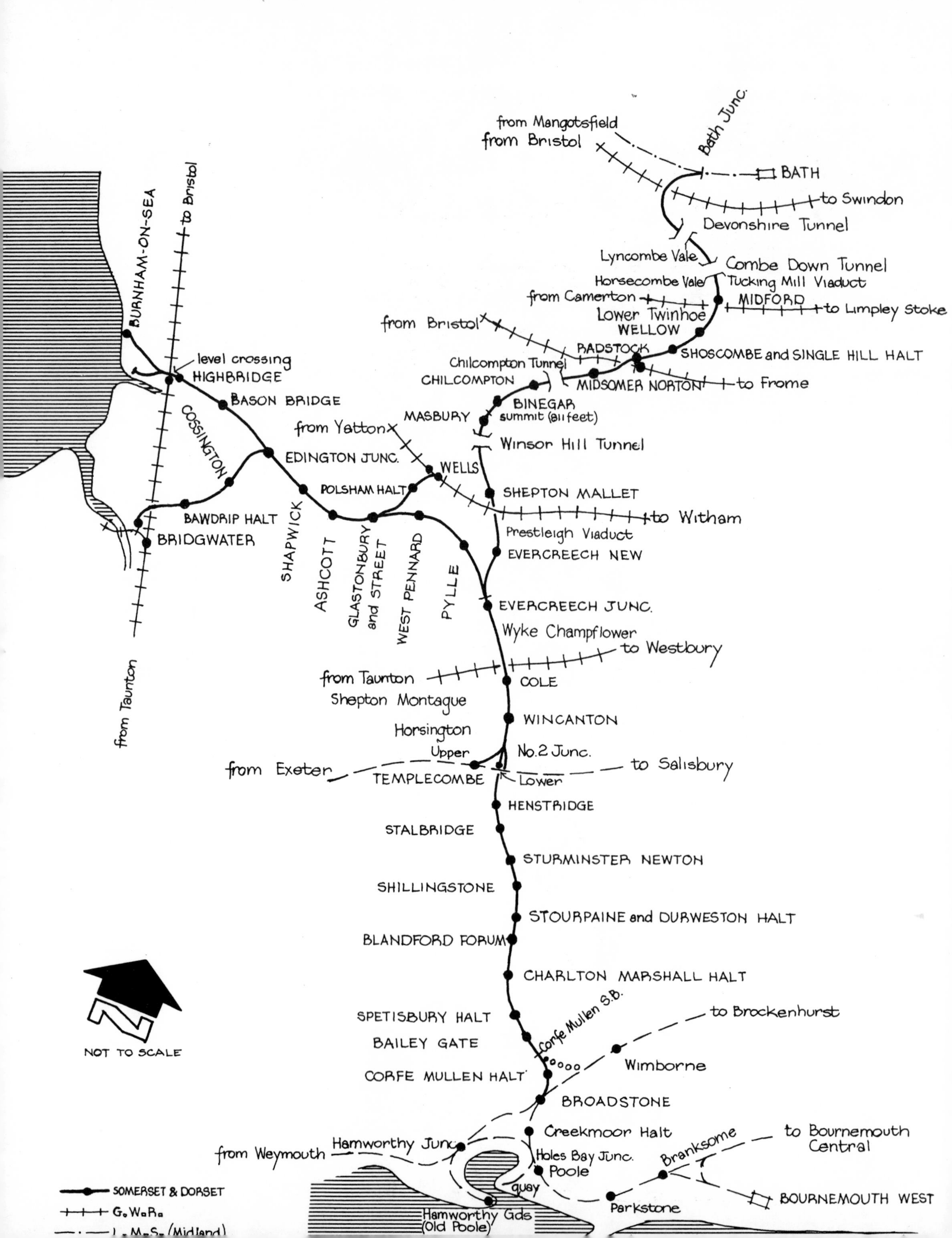

from Mangotsfield
from Bristol
Bath Junc.
BATH
to Swindon
Devonshire Tunnel
Lyncombe Vale
Combe Down Tunnel
Horsecombe Vale
Tucking Mill Viaduct
from Camerton
MIDFORD
to Limpley Stoke
Lower Twinhoe
WELLOW
from Bristol
RADSTOCK
SHOSCOMBE and SINGLE HILL HALT
Chilcompton Tunnel
CHILCOMPTON
MIDSOMER NORTON
to Frome
BINEGAR
MASBURY
summit (811 feet)
from Yatton
Winsor Hill Tunnel
WELLS
SHEPTON MALLET
to Witham
Prestleigh Viaduct
EVERCREECH NEW
EVERCREECH JUNC.
Wyke Champflower
to Westbury
from Taunton
COLE
Shepton Montague
WINCANTON
Horsington
Upper
No.2 Junc.
from Exeter
TEMPLECOMBE
Lower
to Salisbury
HENSTRIDGE
STALBRIDGE
STURMINSTER NEWTON
SHILLINGSTONE
STOURPAINE and DURWESTON HALT
BLANDFORD FORUM
CHARLTON MARSHALL HALT
SPETISBURY HALT
Corfe Mullen S.B.
to Brockenhurst
BAILEY GATE
Wimborne
CORFE MULLEN HALT
BROADSTONE
Creekmoor Halt
to Bournemouth Central
from Weymouth
Hamworthy Junc.
Holes Bay Junc.
Poole
Branksome
quay
Parkstone
BOURNEMOUTH WEST
Hamworthy Gds (Old Poole)
BURNHAM-ON-SEA
to Bristol
level crossing
HIGHBRIDGE
BASON BRIDGE
COSSINGTON
EDINGTON JUNC.
POLSHAM HALT
BAWDRIP HALT
BRIDGWATER
SHAPWICK
ASHCOTT
GLASTONBURY and STREET
WEST PENNARD
PYLLE
from Taunton
NOT TO SCALE
SOMERSET & DORSET
G.W.R.